Everything You Need To Know

JOB HUNTING

A. H. Gort

HarperCollins*Publishers*

**First published in Great Britain in 2001
by HarperCollins Publishers**

Westerhill Road

Bishopbriggs

Glasgow G64 2QT

www.**fire**and**water**.com

© Essential Books 2001

Forms on pp 15 and 28 reproduced by kind
permission of Tameside Metropolitan Borough.
Form B7 on page 47 © Crown copyright 2000,
reproduced by kind permission of
the Department of Social Security.
Form ES5 on pp 162–3 © Crown copyright 2000,
reproduced by kind permission of
the Employment Service

1 3 5 7 9 10 8 6 4 2 0

A catalogue record for this book is available from the
British Library

ISBN 0 00 710232 1

Printed in Great Britain by The Bath Press

CONTENTS

INTRODUCTION

So you need a job, huh? Or then again, maybe you don't. Could be that you're already engaged in perfectly serviceable employment but it's driving you crazy and you're looking to move on.

Whatever your circumstances, the fact that you're reading this right now means that you fit into one of two categories – either you need a job or you want one. After all, you've shelled out your hard-won grant money, redundancy pay, social security handouts or the kids' pocket money and you're expecting this handsome volume to solve all your problems which, of course, it can't do.

What it can do is help you to solve your own problems and give you some advice and encouragement on how to start. It points you in the direction of people and resources to guide you through the process. It draws on real-life examples to show you what you're up against and how other people coped with similar problems. It also contains tips and shortcuts that might just possibly make the whole process a little less painful.

Everything is clearly and concisely laid out with a view to making the information easily digestible. It will prove just as useful to the 16-year-old school leaver as it will to the chief executive of Megacorp Ltd looking for a significant career change.

Now, before we get into it, a few words of warning. Both anecdotal and statistical evidence indicates that getting a job can be a long and arduous process. The chances are that it's going to take longer than you anticipated. There is a strong likelihood that the situation could lead to you becoming demoralised. There may be periods when you get really 'down' and feel like giving up on the whole sorry business of looking for work altogether.

At that point most other books on job hunting have a series of exercises, plans, plots and programmes that you should get to grips with immediately to keep that old black dog at bay.

This book, however, recommends that if anyone tries to burden you with that kind of onerous task, you tell them to shove it. Instead, we suggest that you indulge yourself. Wallow a little. Watch some daytime TV, eat an entire packet of chocolate biscuits or convince someone dead sexy to take you out for dinner. Take some time out from looking for a job and go chuck some bread at some ducks on a pond for the afternoon.

We're working on the assumption that you're serious enough about this job thing to have read this far, right? So, you do want a job. So, you will get one. And when you do, you'll have far less time for engaging in any of the pursuits mentioned above.

Finally, the very best of luck to you in both the pursuit and the practice of the new career that awaits you. We hope we have helped you out and we hope we never have to do so again.

The Web Tip icon alerts you to where relevant website addresses appear in the text. If you are browsing through the book or specifically looking for website information, these icons will take you straight there.

The book is extensively cross-referenced and seeing this icon in the margin will help you to find other information within the book relating to the section you are currently reading.

>> p24
Academic
qualifications

To emphasise a good point, this symbol will appear alongside tips for things you should always remember to do.

To highlight a bad point, this symbol will appear alongside things you should always avoid doing.

Throughout the book, true stories have been used to illustrate the points being made in the main text. These are highlighted by the Real Life icon.

The Basic stuff icon highlights essential information which might sometimes seem so basic as to be patronising, but it would be silly not to include it in a book about job hunting.

Basic stuff

This symbol highlights areas where there is information or tips that will help you to make life easier for yourself or at least avoid potential pitfalls.

help yourself

1

YOUR CLAIM

* ✱ CLAIMING JOBSEEKER'S ALLOWANCE
* ✱ THE JOBSEEKER'S AGREEMENT
* ✱ WHAT YOU WILL GET
* ✱ SIGNING ON
* ✱ HOUSING & COUNCIL BENEFITS
* ✱ OTHER BENEFITS

I care not for work and yet I have no money for champagne.
– John Cooper Clarke

Obviously there's an assumption here that you're unemployed. If you're not, then let's all hope that you never are and encourage you to skip this part completely. If you find yourself unemployed after a period in work, then the chances are you're not feeling too good about things at the moment. The last thing you want to do is start dealing with the grim realities of the daunting bureaucracy down at the 'dole' office, or Benefits Agency as they like to call themselves.

While that's understandable, it's a little on the imprudent side. The faster you get down there and start joining in the battle to get your benefits, the quicker you'll actually get some cash. Please don't for one minute feel guilty about it either. You paid your National Insurance contributions didn't you?

Basic stuff

NATIONAL INSURANCE is a tax collected by the Department of Social Security on behalf of the Inland Revenue from everyone who is working. If you're self-employed you pay it yourself. Otherwise don't worry about it. It's your employer's responsibility to collect it and pass it on. If they don't, they are in big trouble with the tax collector. A percentage of your 'contribution' helps towards funding the National Health Service and the rest is put into a fund that is used to pay benefits. As soon as you leave full-time education you are allocated a National Insurance number that stays with you for the rest of your life and should be used in all official correspondence with the Inland Revenue, Department of Social Security and Benefits Agency. It's a sequence of numbers and letters that looks like this: AB 12 34 56C. If you don't have one – or have lost it – you should contact your local office of the Department of Social Security and they'll sort you out.

And even if you don't pay National Insurance – perhaps you've just left school – you will have to start paying it some time. For the rest of your working life. As your parents did. As their parents did before them. So that money is yours. Go and get it. You will need it. Even if you feel that you may not be entitled to any benefits, it's worth checking. Not only is there the chance of you being pleasantly surprised, but also if you don't register with the Job Centre as unemployed then you will continue to be liable for the aforementioned National Insurance contributions. Which could prove a problem not only in the short term – the Inland Revenue will bill you for them – but in the long term it could also have an effect on your pension. So if you haven't done so already you should sign on at your local Job Centre as soon as you know you are about to become unemployed.

CLAIMING JOBSEEKER'S ALLOWANCE

If you've just upped and left your old job, been sacked for misconduct or recently ceased to be self-employed then you've got a whole heap of problems to face when it comes to claiming any benefits. You will be classed as 'voluntarily unemployed' and as such are ineligible for any Jobseeker's Allowance for the next 26 weeks. You can appeal against that decision. Your case will be referred to a Benefits Agency Adjudicator who will study your circumstances. You will not, however, be entitled to any money during the adjudication process. Hope you've been saving up!

help yourself

STRESS IS AN ILLNESS Being unemployed can be very stressful. Go and see your doctor. Explain that you are out of work and have no income. Stress that this is causing you stress. Perhaps you are not eating or sleeping properly. You may have lost your sex drive. Your self-esteem is low, you suffer mood swings or you find it difficult to deal with everyday tasks. A fair-minded doctor will recognise that preventive treatment is required to keep you healthy and may well declare you unfit for work. The doctor will give you a sick note to prove it. Then you immediately become eligible for Income Support (IS). The regulations on IS are a lot less stringent and you can claim it, along with the other benefits listed below, for 28 weeks. At the end of that period you will be seen by a Benefits Agency doctor. If you fail the 'All Work Test' then your benefit will stop. But don't panic. By this time you will have been unemployed for the statutory 26 weeks and so be eligible for Jobseeker's Allowance. Or, even better, you'll have found a job.

All that anyone else has to do is walk into the nearest Job Centre, find the New Claims section, take a number and make an appointment to see a New Claims Adviser, which usually takes a couple of days. You will also be given a big form called 'Helping You Back To Work' (ES461). That form asks you a whole heap of questions about your circumstances, including full details, usually with proof, of all your financial affairs. These include:

- Savings

- Pensions

- Earnings of other people in your household

- Investments

- Rents due on land or property

- Any part-time work

Be honest. Social Security fraud is a very serious offence and the department employs a considerable number of experts whose job it is to detect any claimant skulduggery. In a worst case scenario, people do go to prison and even in the best case they are liable to return any falsely claimed money.

When it comes to the appointment with the New Claims Adviser it will cut down your waiting time considerably if you have with you some essential details. These are:

1 Your National Insurance number

2 Your P45

3 Your last wage slip

4 Proof of the reason why you left your last job

MEANING WHAT?

A P45 is a document that comes to you from your employer when you leave your job. It details what your earnings in that employment were and what tax you paid. You are supposed to give it to your next employer or to the Benefits Agency if you sign on. If you are leaving full-time education the government will issue you with a P46 instead, which you take along to your first employer. It basically just states that you have yet to pay any tax.

THE JOBSEEKER'S AGREEMENT

Having supplied your details, even before you've discovered whether or not you're entitled to benefit, you'll be asked for other information in order to fill out a Jobseeker's Agreement. Beware. This is not just another form designed to keep the world's rainforests depleted. The Employment Service views this piece of paper as a legally binding contract between you and them. They promise, among other things, to 'always wear a badge' and 'give you advice about employment opportunities'. In return, you agree to be available for work and to 'actively seek work'. You also agree to provide evidence of your jobseeking activities in accordance with a list discussed by you and your adviser.

The temptation here is to say – quite properly – 'I'll do anything. I just want to work.' But it has to be the first rule of any agreement that a contract should be read and fully understood before you sign the thing. Ask if you can take it away and read it before filling it in. That is your right. Remember, they're not giving you any money

TIP

The CAB also gives free advice on debt and consumer issues, benefits, housing, legal matters, employment and immigration.

yet. If there's anything you're unsure of, then your local Citizens' Advice Bureau will cheerfully help you out.

Once you're clear about what you will and won't (or can and can't) do in order to get a job, then go right ahead and fill it in, bearing in mind the following:

1 You will be asked to supply a detailed list every fortnight of who you've rung, who you've written to, which papers you've bought and any other activities you agreed to engage in. Failing to comply can affect your allowance. You can tell them you bought this book for a start!

2 You are asked to list the types of jobs you are looking for. Each job has a code number and these codes are put into a computer along with your other details. When you see your adviser every subsequent fortnight, they will punch in your details and see if a job in any of the categories you stated has become available. They can tell you to apply for that job. Failing to comply can affect your allowance. So don't go saying you want a job as an air stewardess if you get dizzy wearing high heels!

TIP

If you've found an adviser particularly helpful, ask if you can see them regularly.

3 If you go for a job interview as directed by your adviser, or for one that you found in the Job Centre (the details are entered into the computer each time you enquire about a position advertised there), and you turn the job down, it can affect your benefit. And don't go thinking you can deliberately sabotage the interview either. If the Employment Service checks – as it is wont to do – and finds out, it can suspend your benefit.

WHAT YOU WILL GET

If, after taking into consideration your stocks and shares, gilt-edged securities and string of penthouse flats, you are deemed poor enough to qualify for benefits, you will in due course receive a giro cheque, although you can if you so wish have the money paid directly into your bank account. Worth considering if you fancy one of the post office staff and don't want them to know you're on your uppers.

It will be an alarmingly small amount of money. Believe me. Get a job. Fast. Without going into the labyrinthine details of all the different entitlements it's worth looking at just one example.

A single person aged over 25 with no dependants in the summer of 2000 was entitled to £51.40 per week. This, you will be assured in the notification letter, is how much money the law says you need to live on each week.

TIP

Your benefits can be affected if you turn up late to sign on.

The money you get as Jobseeker's Allowance will come to you every fortnight within two or three days of signing on. You are, of course, perfectly entitled to blow the whole lot on champagne if you so wish. However, it's worth knowing that if, in order to do so, you stop paying your bills, then a lot of people – mainly the utilities – can apply to the Department of Social Security to have the money deducted at source from your allowance.

SIGNING ON

TIP

One of the few valid reasons for being unavailable at a specific time is religious grounds.

Signing on entails going down to the Job Centre every two weeks at a prearranged time and on a particular day to spend some time with your adviser. Turn up. And don't be late. Failure to turn up can affect your allowance. If for some reason you can't make it – most likely you've got a job interview – contact them to explain why. Always write down the name of the person you spoke to.

OFF THE RECORD

I'm not being funny, but some of the people who work here see the claimants as idle scum who are just trying to dodge working. Most of the staff are fair-minded, but it seems to me some of them are looking for ways to give the claimants a hard time. My advice, if you can't make it to sign on for whatever reason, is to come in beforehand if possible and explain why. Make sure your details get entered into the computer and make a note of their name. If you phone up, some of them may not bother to let anyone know because they know your claim will get put on hold. And if you do have any trouble when you're dealing with a particular adviser, ask if you can see someone else. Someone who 'understands your circumstances better' is usually a good one.

A N Benefits adviser

HOUSING & COUNCIL BENEFITS

After making your new claim at the Job Centre, your next task is to get yourself down to the Town Hall or Council Offices Housing Department. And it's a good job you've no place of work to go to because you've a busy day ahead of you. Armed with notification from the Department of Social Security that you are eligible for Jobseeker's Allowance, you are now entitled to claim Housing Benefit and Council Tax relief. Like the previous lot, they will ask you for detailed financial information. And again, please don't lie. Housing Benefit fraud is just as serious an offence, and most councils employ a considerable number of experts whose job it is to root out any shenanigans and prosecute any serious offenders. In some cases people do go to jail and in all cases they have to give the money back.

TIP
Refusal to broaden your availability and job search will affect your benefits.

If you do qualify for Housing Benefit it will be paid to you in full or part by a cheque each month, or again you can choose to have it paid straight into your bank account. A third option is to have it sent directly to your landlord. That's a very good option to take if you think you may be tempted to spend the money on champagne.

If you own your own home then things could get sticky for a time. While there is provision for you to claim at least part of your mortgage repayments, the rules are complex and the process lengthy. Obviously, it is to be hoped that you made provision for a period of unemployment when you took out the insurance on your mortgage.

If you qualify in full or part for Council Tax relief, then the bit of the council that gives rebates will give it directly to the bit of the council that collects the taxes, thereby removing all temptation to spend the money on champagne.

OTHER BENEFITS

Once you join the ranks of the dignified unemployed, there are some other things you and your family can get as a result of the government saving up your National Insurance contributions. They include:

- Free dental care
- Free prescriptions

Tameside
Metropolitan Borough

Exchequer & Customer Services
Benefits Section
Council Offices, Wellington Road,
Ashton-under-Lyne, Tameside OL6 6DL
Telephone 0161 342 8355
Minicom 0161 342 3839
Fax 0161 342 3876
www.tameside.gov.uk

ASHTON-UNDER-LYNE · AUDENSHAW · DENTON · DROYLSDEN · DUKINFIELD · HYDE · LONGDENDALE · MOSSLEY · STALYBRIDGE

APPLICATION FOR
HOUSING BENEFIT AND/OR COUNCIL TAX BENEFIT
Private and confidential

Name:

Address:

Postcode:

Email address:

Telephone No:

Local Authority use only:
Date Stamp

আপনে অগ্রেঝ ভাষা,বাঝবানী ই লখবানী তঙহীঙ
হীথ তী মহેઠભানী হয় ટેহমসায়ড ম্রহাটিনসল ব্যাস
থাবলী ইন্টেরপ্রিটর-ট্রান্সলেটর সর্ভিসনী নীઝીના
সংস্থামে সংপর্ক সাধী।

ઠাહিউিঝ બেইড সেন্ટর:
પ৬ বারিংটন স্ট্রীট
আঠঝন-অটઝર-বাহিন।
টেবিঝীন: 0161-342 3604

0161-342 2807

তথ্য দেওয়ার কাগজ বা ফর্ম

কিছু তথ্য আনার জন্য এই কাগজটিক ইংরাঝীঠিক কিছু
প্রশ্ন করা হয়েঝে। এখুনি নুঝাঝত আপনার যদি কোনও
রকম অসুবিধা হয় তাহলে পীঝের ঠিকানায় যোগাযোগ
করুন।

টি এম বি সি, ইন্টারপ্রটর ট্রান্সলেটর সার্ভিস,
৫৬, ঝাারিংটন স্ট্রীট, আ্যশটন আন্ডার লাইন।
টেলিফোন: 0161-342 2806

If you have any information on suspected
Housing or Council Tax Benefit fraud ring:

Fraud Hotline
0800 9178179

Information will be treated in strict confidence.

Awarded for excellence   INVESTOR IN PEOPLE

Your claim will be assessed for both Housing and Council Tax Benefit (if applicable). Please note if you pay your rent to Manchester Council, you will need to claim Housing Benefit from them.

Are you a:
Please tick the appropriate box.

Private Tenant ☐   Owner Occupier ☐

Housing Association ☐   Crown Tenant ☐
Tenant

Housing Benefit reference number (if you know it) ....

Council Tax account number (if you know it)................................

Are you the only person over the age of 18 living in this property?

Yes ☐   No ☐

If **yes**, we may be able to award a Single Person Discount.

You will lose money if you do not return this form immediately. Do not delay! If you do not have all the information we are asking for, send the application form to us now and supply the remaining information within 28 days.
All the details you give will be treated in the strictest confidence.

Return your application form to:

Exchequer & Customer Services
Benefits Section
Tameside MBC
Council Offices, Wellington Road
Ashton-under-Lyne, Tameside OL6 6DL

Alternatively you can hand it in at your local Customer Service Centre where help in completing the form is available if required.

ILLUSTRATION 1   Typical local authority application form for Housing and/or Council Tax Benefit

- Free eye tests

- Help towards the cost of spectacles

- Free school meals

- Free milk for pregnant women and children under five

- Travel cost to hospital

- Free wigs

- Help with prison visits

So a lot of fun to be had there if you come from a family of balding, myopic burglars. If you find yourself in extremely dire straits, then there is such a thing as a 'Crisis Loan' available, the definition of which is as follows:

'A repayable interest-free loan to help people who cannot meet their immediate short-term expenses in an emergency or following a disaster to prevent serious damage or risk to the health or safety of them, or a member of their family.'

Nothing in there about needing it to back a hot tip for the 3.30 at Aintree, so don't even think about it. Bear in mind also that it's a loan. The Benefits Agency will claw it back through your biweekly giro payments.

It is possible also to claim for travel expenses and overnight accommodation for any job interview out of the area if the potential employer isn't picking up the tab. You'd be hard pressed to get a flight to Barbados to inquire about bar work, but reasonable claims are dealt with quickly.

Huge rafts of leaflets on all of the above are always available from the Department of Social Security. Once again, the lovely people at the Citizens' Advice Bureau are on hand to help you deal with the forms and advise you if you get stuck.

Finally on this point, remember that the unemployment figures and their reduction are a constant thorn in the side of any government of the day. As a direct result of the pain thereby inflicted, highly motivated teams of civil servants and advisers are constantly looking for ways to reform this area, which now applies directly to you.

This means that the rules can and will constantly change. No matter how diligent we may have been in ensuring that what is contained here is correct, you must make sure that you get the very latest up-to-date information. If you do come unstuck, then get straight down to the Citizens' Advice Bureau.

HOW I GOT THE JOB: *Nepotism! My mother has worked there for years and years. She was always saying, 'Why don't you get a proper job?' So I thought maybe I could give it a go and still carry on working as a DJ – which I do. My mum gave me an address for me to send my CV to and they got back to me within a couple of weeks to arrange an interview. I had done it before as a summer job during my A-level years, so that helped. I was interviewed by a panel of three people. I really hate doing interviews because they're such a pressurised situation, but I decided before I went in that there was no point putting on a show. I dressed how I normally dress and was just myself. And they loved me. As everybody does and should.*

Michael, benefits administrator (and part-time DJ)

Probably the most entertaining website on the subject of your rights as a benefit claimant is at **www.urban75.com**. The site is run by a bunch of cheeky rascals who don't on the whole approve of the concept of work. As you enter their site you'll notice lots of material about environmental activism, going to raves and other related issues. If that's your bag, then fine, enjoy yourself. The less anarchical should go straight to the 'Rights' icon where you'll find a section entitled *Jobseeker's Allowance Survival Guide*. It offers a plain-speaking and comprehensive description of the ins and outs of the claiming procedure, details of your rights and some handy tips on ensuring that you don't get pushed around the system.

READ THIS
Welfare Benefits Handbook. Published by the Child Poverty Action Group. Reference only

Wow. What a book. Big and chunky, it was written by a team of 13 rights experts and covers everything anyone could ever need to know about the subject of claiming benefits. It includes very clear, step-by-step guides for every stage of the claiming procedure, from leaving work to getting back to work. It also looks as if it would be indispensable if you ever get into trouble with the Benefits Agency or need to challenge a decision.

NO WAY!

DON'T feel guilty about claiming benefits

DON'T delay in getting down to the Benefits Agency

DON'T lie about anything when making your claim

DON'T expect to be able to live off your benefits for very long

DON'T fill in the Jobseeker's Agreement without careful thought

WAY TO GO!

DO make sure you got your P45 from your last employer

DO take all relevant information with you

DO seek advice from an independent adviser if you're confused

DO tell the Benefits Agency if you can't make an appointment

DO if you're a homeowner contact your mortgage provider ASAP

GO YOUR OWN WAY!

- You choose how you have your benefits paid to you

- You can use the standard form for your job search or supply your own

- A Crises Loan is available in an emergency but it will have to be repaid

- You can pay some outstanding bills directly from your benefits

- Income Support is sometimes more relevant than Jobseeker's Allowance

TEN TASKS TICKED OFF

Got my P45 from my last job ❏

Made a comprehensive list of all my property,
    assets and savings ❏

Been to the Job Centre and made a new claim ❏

Read the Job Seeker's Agreement ❏

Sought independent expert advice ❏

Filled it in and signed it ❏

Been to the Council Offices and claimed for
    Housing Benefit and Council Tax ❏

Asked the Benefits Agency about my other entitlements ❏

Filled in all those forms ❏

Got myself a cup of tea and a chocolate biscuit. I deserve it ❏

2
COPING WITH
UNEMPLOYMENT

✳ CLAIMING & LEARNING

✳ WHICH COURSE IS BEST?

✳ WHAT FUNDING IS AVAILABLE?

✳ HOW MUCH TIME WILL IT TAKE?

I would rather be a quantity surveyor. I don't know what they do, but it sounds like a proper job. – Arthur Smith

Okay. The government has given you all this lovely money to spend. They're paying the rent and you've rushed round to get your teeth filled and bifocals updated. Now what?

Well, one of the first things you might want to look at is the issue of education. Not only do you now have the time to pursue those subjects which have always fascinated you but if you're canny you may well hit on a course that improves your job-hunting prospects. Plus which, pretty well all of these splendid learning opportunities are available to you free of charge if you're in receipt of benefits.

Let's take a look at the issue of education and the unemployed first of all. Once again, if you're still in work you can skip this bit.

CLAIMING & LEARNING

Basically the rule is that you can study for anything up to 16 hours a week and remain in receipt of Jobseeker's Allowance. You do have to tell the Benefits Agency what you're doing. Remember that you've signed an agreement which states that you are available for and actively seeking full-time employment. Busting through that 16-hour rule immediately categorises you as a full-time student and renders you ineligible for Jobseeker's Allowance. If the training or education you settle on is specifically designed to further your job prospects then you should find the advisers at the Job Centre positively encouraging.

In fact if you're just vaguely wondering what courses are available and what the implications of joining them are, then the Job Centre should probably be your first port of call. They carry full details on all local schemes and courses along with accompanying literature. They may well direct you to one of the many local Training Enterprise Centres (TECs) or career advice bodies that have blossomed, particularly in areas of high unemployment.

Whether you are in or out of work there are a couple of things that you really do have to think about before you settle on any kind of course. Let's deal with the three fundamentals in sections.

WHICH COURSE IS BEST?

To a large extent the answer to that question will be influenced by the other two factors of time and money. But there are other considerations to be taken into account. In the first instance let's not forget that the purpose of this book is to get you a job. So we'll be concentrating on that aspect to a greater extent.

The first thing you need to know is what kind of job you want at the end of all this training. It's pointless taking a cake-making course at night school if you've got your heart set on running a diet and fitness centre for example. In chapter 4 we'll be looking at ways for you to decide on a career, but for argument's sake let's just for now suppose you know what you want to do and move on to the second issue.

Which is what course will best help you get that job. Obviously there are a lot of different kinds of jobs out there and as many, if not more, courses. It would take a big book to match them all up with each other. This is not that book. However, it can offer you some practical tips.

First off, talk to other people who do the job you want. Three little questions should do it:

1 What qualifications did they need to get?

2 What qualifications do they think they should have got to further their prospects?

3 Did they waste any time gaining qualifications that proved to be useless?

If you can't find out from someone you know – perhaps you want to be a lion tamer – then it may be time to talk to some sort of careers adviser. The Job Centre is a good place to start down that road. As is Yellow Pages. Local libraries also usually have a whole reference section on careers and education. If you find your mind boggled by the sheer weight of information then grab hold of a librarian and explain to them exactly what you want. They are trained to access the most relevant information at high speed.

Another option is to speak to an educational establishment. Just go along to the nearest college of further education and ask if you can see someone about the courses on offer. Colleges and universities get funding proportional to the number of students they attract. So a new one is worth a few quid to them. They should be bending over backwards to get you enrolled.

OFF THE RECORD

There can be a tendency in some of the newer, more commercially minded universities to bend the rules slightly to get high numbers of students enrolled just to secure their funding. Particularly with mature students on what you might say are the 'more esoteric' postgraduate courses. If you aren't interviewed, or are interviewed in a half-hearted fashion, then alarm bells should perhaps be ringing about the quality of the course.

A N Admissions tutor

Next you need to consider what level of learning you're ready for. Presumably there's not much point taking A-level lion-taming classes if you haven't yet fully mastered basic whip-cracking. So here's a brief guide to the most common types of learning available to you, starting with the most straightforward:

● Basic and essential skills

● Life-enhancing classes

● Academic qualifications

● Access courses

● Vocational qualifications

BASIC AND ESSENTIAL SKILLS

What used to be called the 'three Rs' comes under this category: reading, writing and arithmetic. What a pity the deviser of that statement never learnt to spell. Which is also a basic skill. It really covers anything you need to go about your daily life. It doesn't necessarily mean you're stupid either. It could be that you're out of practice or that 'basic and essential skills' have moved on since you last looked at them. Take a look at this list:

● Reading

● Writing

● Spelling

● Handwriting

● Arithmetic

● Using computers

● Filling in forms

● Basic English

These are the things that are most likely to be taught by a local college or adult learning centre as 'basic and essential' skills. Aside from helping you brush up on lost or neglected areas, these courses are useful in so far as they act as an induction into the whole learning process. Many of them are structured in such a way that they will lead on to other courses and qualifications.

LIFE-ENHANCING CLASSES

These are probably best typified by the good old-fashioned 'evening class' run at your local school or community centre and covering a host of subjects of varying degrees of usefulness to the jobseeker. Courses are usually short, informal and not too demanding. They are particularly good for learning languages and many of them are run as proper recognised courses with appropriate qualifications. It's also a great way to get back into the swing of learning if you've been away from it for some time.

TIP

Life-enhancing classes are those you take because you want to rather than have to.

Aside from the local education authority a host of classes are run by the Workers' Educational Association. The WEA was set up in 1903 as a philanthropic endeavour to provide an education for adults who had no other way of getting one.

Today it's a national organisation with hundreds of branches offering part-time classes in a myriad of subjects. The classes are designed to develop your learning skills and understanding rather than get you qualified, but don't let that stop you from enquiring. They don't charge much and all the courses are taught by professionals in their field. The phone book will carry details of the nearest branch to you.

ACADEMIC QUALIFICATIONS

Basically there are three levels of academic qualification available in pretty much any subject and they are:

- GCSE
- A level
- University degree

The GCSE (General Certificate of Secondary Education) is the one that most people take before they leave school. If you never did, or you want to take more, then courses are widely available through most colleges of further education and some schools. You can take as many as you want simultaneously or consecutively and each one takes an academic year to complete with a written (sometimes oral and practical as well) examination at the end.

In Scotland, of course, educational qualifications are slightly different, with Highers instead of A levels, for example, but the same basic advice still applies.

help yourself

YOU DON'T HAVE TO GO to any school or college to pass GCSE examinations. You can do it all by yourself. Just find out where your local examination board is based and ask them to send you details of the rules, syllabus and timetable for your chosen subject and you can study at your leisure. It helps if you can get hold of the 'Examiners' Reports', which detail exactly what they're looking for in the final exam. You will also have to contact the board to make arrangements to take the exam under 'examination conditions'.

The A level is the harder version of the GCSE. Adults are normally expected to complete A levels within a year, but if that looks like too big a task then check with the college about splitting it over two years. They can do that sometimes. A levels are usually the qualifications that school leavers require to get into university.

The degree is the hardest of them all. It generally takes three years and involves continual assessment of your progress as well as a series of examinations in most cases. (Although you can get an 'honorary degree' from a university for doing nothing at all other than being famous.) There's a lot of reading, lectures and course work to complete and it usually all takes place at a university, although of course you can do a degree course through the Open University.

If you're a mature student and fancy a crack at a university degree course but haven't got any GCSE or A-level qualifications, don't despair. A lot of universities are prepared to be flexible and will enrol older students on the basis of their 'appropriate life skills' or in other words what you learned in the 'university of life'. The person to speak to at the university is the 'admissions tutor'. They'll really be looking out for whether or not you're committed to the three years of study and what your chances of qualifying are.

If it looks like you won't be able to enrol on the basis of your previous experience, or you are nervous about plunging straight into the world of academia after a long lay-off, then the next bit about 'access courses' may be useful to you.

While getting a degree is liable to open up more employment opportunities, it won't of course guarantee you a job. In a lot of cases it is actually the first step in a career. Getting a law degree for example doesn't entitle you to practise law, it's merely the entry

TIP
Employers increasingly ask to see proof of qualifications before they'll give you a job.

requirement which enables you to start studying to be a lawyer. Same with teaching. You get a degree and then you attend teacher training classes.

Choosing a degree and a place to study at is a big deal. It is going to take at least three years out of your life and may entail major upheavals, possibly even moving to a different town. So do choose carefully. Here's a few tips to help you through that decision:

- All universities have a website these days. Take a look around that.

- Try to find the unofficial website actually run by the students. That will give you the inside dope on both the town and the college.

- Visit the campus during term time and have a good look around.

- Talk to the other students.

- If you attend an interview remember that they are on trial too. You need to be totally happy that you can learn there.

ACCESS COURSES

Short for 'access to higher education or university'. These courses are specifically designed for people over 21 with no recognised qualifications who want to return to learning.

In addition to making the learning environment as flexible and friendly as possible they also pay specific attention to the practical needs of students. So timetables will be arranged around working times for those in employment and school times for working parents. Most of them have crèche and childcare facilities on campus as well.

Many access courses also have a deal with a university which guarantees a number of automatic places on degree courses. Again the library or your local education authority is the place to research information on access courses near you.

VOCATIONAL QUALIFICATIONS

As in stuff you learn that is directly useful to you in a specific job. Usually these courses put more emphasis on the practical aspects of actually working in a field than they do on paper qualifications. There are a bewildering array of vocational courses and qualifications available and most of them are abbreviated just to make life more complex.

Many of these courses, while not essential, are highly valued by employers and the more enlightened among them will be prepared not only to release you from work to be trained up, they'll foot the bill for the fees as well.

If you're reading this book because you're looking for a job then obviously a vocational qualification is a good thing to get. Be advised however that many employers will insist that as part of their agreement to send you on a course they expect you to commit to their firm or organisation for a period of time. Your boss, in other words, doesn't want to foot the bill for making you smarter so that you can go to work for a competitor.

TIP
A vocational course is usually known as an NVQ (national vocational qualification).

WHAT FUNDING IS AVAILABLE?

If you are working already, or are moving from one form of education into another, then any course will have to be paid for. Local night classes may run to only a few quid a session but a full-time three-year degree can run to several thousand pounds. Local authority grants are available in some cases to help defray some or all of those fees. That tends to apply mainly to those who are embarking on a full-time education, mind you. Evening classes for example will not be covered.

If you are intending to go to college on a full-time basis then swing by the Council Offices and ask for the information and forms. They are big forms and you'll be asked for very detailed financial information along with proof of all sources of income including any investments or interest payments, all of which will have to be certified.

Basically any grants that are available are designed to cover tuition fees and living costs. You already know from the number of students you encounter on a daily basis working in bars, restaurants and bookshops that the amount you will be expected to live on will be small. So prepare for some belt-tightening exercises.

CERTIFICATION =OF= INCOME

IMPORTANT

These forms may be used to obtain evidence
of income to support an application for
student grants and loans.

They are intended to be used as alternatives to the
Original Certificates (e.g. P.60, Bank/Building Society
Interest Statements etc).

They must be authorised by the employer,
bank or building society before being
returned to the Student Awards Service Unit.

ILLUSTRATION 2   Local authority student grant applications require vast amounts of information

FORM 1(a)

**TAMESIDE METROPOLITAN BOROUGH
EDUCATION AND LEISURE SERVICES
STUDENT AWARDS SERVICE UNIT**

PRIVATE AND CONFIDENTIAL

CONFIRMATION OF INCOME

PART 'A' (to be completed by parents of dependent student or husband/wife of independent student). **SEE NOTES 1 AND 2 OVERLEAF.**

Name and Address of Student..
(BLOCK CAPITALS)

....

....

Name of Employee..

Employee Reference Number..

PART 'B' to be completed by employer(s) or a responsible officer of the employing organisation. **SEE NOTES ON COMPLETION OF THIS FORM OVERLEAF.**

Gross Annual Income. I certify that the following payments were made to the undermentioned employee during the financial year ended 5th April 2000.

Name of Employee _____

(i) **Total Gross Income** — including commission, bonus, overtime and sickness benefit **(before deduction of superannuation)** ....

Value of other emoluments e.g. free quarters, meals etc. ....

1999/2000 Tax Code		**TOTAL**	

(ii) The above-named employee *is/is not a Partner or a Director of this Company.

(iii) Total superannuation contributions paid during the year (excluding National Insurance Contributions) **included** in above total £ _____

(iv) If not employed for the whole financial year please specify dates of employment.

From.. To ....

Signed.. Name of Firm ....

Position in Firm .... Address..

Date.. ....

....

*Delete as applicable

EMPLOYER'S OFFICIAL STAMP

32211

Basic stuff

Your local education authority is also responsible for disbursing money in the shape of student loans, which are exactly what they sound like. Loans for students. How much you get depends on your course, where you live and where you study. For the academic year 2000/01 the maximum loan available outside London was £3,725 for a full year.

THE ACADEMIC OR 'LEARNING' YEAR runs from September through to June in practically all cases. Which means that July and August are when you should start exploring courses, finding funding and actually turning up to enrol.

The money is paid to you in three instalments, which is good for budgeting purposes, and yes of course you are supposed to give it back. The good news on that is that you are not liable to start repaying it until the April after you have finished your whole course, provided that you are in work and earning more than £10,000 per year.

Once you are working, the amount you have to cough up each month is based on your income and deducted directly from your pay packet by your employer who gives it to the Inland Revenue, which in turn pays the student loan company.

While local education authority grants and student loans are the two main sources of funding available to those in full-time education there are other lumps of money to be found if you look hard enough. Here's a brief rundown of some probable sources:

CAREER DEVELOPMENT LOANS (CDL)

This is a fund set up by the Department for Education and Employment (DfEE) to loan out money for those who want to take vocational courses. In other words you have to prove that it will lead to improved employment opportunities. The loan is available to anyone over 18 who has no access to any other funding and you can borrow up to eight grand. You pay it back through one of the banks involved in the scheme when the course is finished and payments can be deferred until you start work.

The CDL people have a free information line on 0800 585 505 where you can get further details.

TEACHER TRAINING COURSES

A new scheme designed to encourage people into the teaching profession. For training in certain key subjects you not only get your fees waived but also the government will give you a five grand incentive. Local education authorities have been given the responsibility of dishing out the dosh so check with them for applications and copies of the rules.

EDUCATION MAINTENANCE ALLOWANCE

At the time of writing this one was available from only a select number of local education authorities. It's for school leavers only and designed to keep you in education. It is based on your parents' income – they will have to fill in huge forms with full financial details – and will get you up to £30 a week, plus end-of-term bonuses for good attendance and making good progress.

INDIVIDUAL LEARNING ACCOUNT

Not so much a source of funding as a discount scheme run by the DfEE. You have to be over 19 and not eligible for any other type of funding. It's kind of like joining a club really. You get a membership card and number which entitles you to some benefits including the option to pay for education by instalments and to apply for between 20 and 80 per cent discounts on certain courses. The free phone number for more information is 0800 100 900. This is a useful number for information on all course funding and employment training opportunities. It belongs to Learning Direct, a helpline set up in 1998 offering up-to-date and accurate information on the whole world of learning.

TIP
Once studying you can apply to the Student Union for a 'Hardship Loan' in an emergency.

TRAINING AND ENTERPRISE COUNCIL

These are local bodies set up by the government to address local employment and training issues. It may well be that your trail from the Job Centre has already led you to your local TEC. If not, they are in the phone book. Sometimes they have money available for certain types of training. Certainly the most clued-up among them will be able to give you guidance on other sources of funding.

DISABLED STUDENT ALLOWANCES

For those with disabilities or specific learning difficulties (dyslexia for example) there is money available for help with any specialist equipment you may need, any non-medical help – sign language interpreters for instance – and a general allowance to cover costs of books and travel. You apply via your local education authority.

DEPENDENT CHILDREN'S ALLOWANCE

If you're a single parent or there are other members of your family dependent on you for money then the local education authority can award you an allowance to help feed and clothe them while you study.

OTHER GRANTS AND BURSARIES

Charities, trade unions, trust funds and philanthropists can prove to be a source of money for a variety of courses. The library is the place to research these. A useful contact is the Educational Grants Advisory Service. Send an SAE to 501/505 Kingsland Road, London E8 4AU for further details.

HOW MUCH TIME WILL IT TAKE?

As we have already seen, there are a host of courses and they can be fitted into a myriad different lifestyles. So you're going to have to take a close look at yours to see just what suits you best.

There are however a couple of things you should bear in mind.

Primary among those things is your 'stickability'. Specifically if you are training for a qualification, a half-finished course really is more of a waste of time and effort than doing nothing at all. So be absolutely sure before you embark on this journey that you have the time, stamina and resources to see it through to the end.

Beware also of looking at any timetable of lessons and thinking that just because you have to attend a college for a few hours a week that the rest is leisure time. Nothing could be further from the truth. Time spent in class is just the beginning of the story. The following are more than likely to be included in the overall picture:

- Course work

- Written essays

- Projects and special assignments

- Field trips

- Private study

- Reading

- Tutorials

- Revision

- Exams

If you have plumped for a full-time course then rest assured it will live up to its description. It is estimated that many students spend more hours working weekly on their degree courses than they do when they graduate into the workplace. In order to take it all in – especially if you are returning to education – you are going to have to be organised, self-disciplined and determined. You are also going to need the support of family and loved ones.

The time that you spend studying is also time that you are not spending on directly getting a job. So if you are looking for work at the same time, that will have to be factored into the equation. It may well be that the only work you are able to get is typical lowly-paid student-type work. Which will of course also make demands on your time.

HOW I GOT THE JOB: *I knew that bar work was the best option but I didn't want to work anywhere that was either full of gangsters, played horrible techno music or you had to dress like a tart. I went round all the bars until I found one where I really felt comfortable and started hanging out there. I used to make a real effort to dress smartly and be friendly with the staff. Then when I knew the proprietor a bit I asked if he had any work. He didn't. But I kept coming in and pestering him. I left my number, stressed I could start any time and was prepared to work shifts. Eventually when he did have a vacancy I think I must've sprung immediately to mind.*

Kelly, part-time waitress and student

Real
LIFE

If, having weighed up all of the above, done your research and your sums, you decide to go for further education then a whole new world of exciting and stimulating opportunity awaits you. An education can lead you into jobseeking areas that never dawned on you or never seemed possible before. That's in addition to the useful stuff you're going to learn, the new friends and new experiences you're going to enjoy.

WEB TIP

One of the undisputed kings of education and training advice is the Hobson Group. They publish each year a series of massive books which are also hugely expensive. Their *Postgraduate Directory*, for example, is £109.99. Fortunately they also have pretty much all you need to know on their website at www.Hobsons.com. While this is a vast site it is very easy to get around and organised so that you can search by subject and establishment. The establishments cover every style of educational emporium with links to their individual sites. Likewise the list of subjects takes in everything from GCSEs in accountancy to PhDs in zoology. They also deal with studying overseas, training courses for those in work and carry some useful graduate recruitment information.

READ THIS

UCAS Guide. Published in association with the *Independent* newspaper. £19.95

This is a big, thick book. However it is published by the people who should know what they're talking about. UCAS stands for Universities and Colleges Admissions Service. They're the people who administer the process of enrolling into further education. Their book, which is updated annually, lists over 30,000 courses running throughout the UK. It also carries details from all the main universities on what their interviewing processes are, when their open days are, entry requirements and campus locations.

NO WAY!

DON'T go rushing into an unsuitable course

DON'T walk before you can run. Consider access courses

DON'T be deterred by a lack of formal qualifications

DON'T expect a qualification to guarantee you a job

DON'T give up before you've completed the course

WAY TO GO!

DO, if you're signing on, tell the Benefits Agency about your training plans

DO think about what kind of job you want to be trained for

DO ask other people what training was useful for their job

DO make sure you apply for grants and loans in plenty of time

DO call Learning Direct on 0800 100 900

GO YOUR OWN WAY!

● Teach yourself or try the Open University

● You can get training while working. Speak to your employer

● The Workers' Educational Association may not be glamorous, but it is brilliant at teaching stuff

● Look for flexibility. Ask if a course can be taken over a longer period

TEN TASKS TICKED OFF

Asked my friends about their qualifications ❏

Talked to the people at the Job Centre ❏

Phoned Learning Direct on 0800 100 900 ❏

Spent some time in the library ❏

Visited the nearest and best educational establishment ❏

Did my sums to see if I can afford the time and money ❏

Picked out a course ❏

Went along and enrolled ❏

Applied for grants and loans ❏

Practised dancing badly to very loud music. I deserve it ❏

3

STAYING
SOLVENT

✳ BUDGETING

✳ SAVING MONEY

✳ MAKING MONEY

✳ DECLARING INCOME

✳ COPING WITH DEBT

I'm doing okay. I've got enough money to last me for the rest of me life. Provided I drop dead in the next ten minutes. – Bob Dillinger

Let's get down and dirty here. Unless you've been a very wise virgin and salted heaps of boodle away, you are going to be skint or at least skinter than you were when you were working. Which is painful enough but if you're not careful the ramifications may even affect your pocket when you resume employment.

That's not to say that it's all bad news. As well as helping you avoid some of the pitfalls of penury, we hope this chapter will give some tips on how to make extra cash, and how to live pretty well for a lot less money.

Of course you may feel that you're sitting pretty with a nice big fat redundancy payment gathering interest in the building society. Let's hope so. Nevertheless you're still going to have to think carefully about how long it's going to last and what it's supposed to pay for. This is not really a book about financial management, so you might want to seek some alternative advice on how best to make a lump sum work for you. Don't go blowing it though. Well, probably a good idea to blow some of it. Earmark a sensible amount for deployment as 'mad money', head for the champagne shop and when you've recovered, read this next bit.

BUDGETING

If you have got advance notice of impending unemployment, then it's best to get cracking on a plan immediately. The sooner you put the moves in place the easier it will be down the line. And the first thing to do is sit down with your partner and/or family to explain exactly what's going down. Much better that they're braced now for a little bit of belt-tightening than it takes them unawares later.

The second potential benefit of this approach is that with some rejigging of work and domestic duties it may be possible to maintain the status quo for the household accounts. Put simply, that means if your partner takes on extra earning duties you may have to cop for the cooking *and* the washing up. Whatever comes and goes, everyone in the house is going to have to be flexible and understanding. Which is why they all need to be involved in your next task, the drawing up of a current monthly household budget.

We're talking a big list here of everything that comes in and out. Mainly out. Most people know what they've got, they just don't know where it goes. You must be scrupulously honest and you must be exact to the nearest penny. No good saying, 'We spend maybe a hundred on champagne every month.' As we shall see later it is important that it all gets accounted for.

Obviously it is impossible for anyone else to try to guess what would be on your household list. Everyone is different, so don't copy this one, you'll have to use it as a jumping-off point. However, what is important are the categories of outgoings. Notice that these are in four groups. The Consumer Credit Counselling Service categorises these groups as follows:

TIP
How much redundancy money you get depends on how long you've worked, your age and what your wages were.

BUDGET SHEET

INCOME	£		EXPENDITURE	£
Salary			Council Tax	
Interest payments			Mortgage/rent	
State benefits	**1**	Water rates	
Share dividends			Gas	
Rents received			Electricity	
			TV licence	
			Clothing	
		2	Food	
			Housekeeping	
			Credit cards	
		3	Loan repayments	
			Hire purchase	
			Walking around	
			Telephone	
			Alcohol	
			Cigarettes	
		4	Birthdays/Christmas	
			Entertainment	
			Holiday	
			Hobbies	
TOTAL			**TOTAL**	

ILLUSTRATION 3   Your budget sheet may look a little like this

1 **Priority payments** These are the things that you absolutely, positively must pay to remain out of trouble. It's a matter of keeping a roof over your head, your essential utilities connected and not getting into trouble with the authorities. Although not on the list above you would also need to include any fines or outstanding county court judgments, plus any outstanding sums owed to the Inland Revenue or Customs and Excise for VAT arrears.

2 **Basic living costs** Food, medicines, clothing, school dinners, cleansing products etc. Anything which keeps you alive really.

3 **Other creditors** Theseare people to whom you may owe money but the law figures they have less of a claim than the first group. You should really make a separate list of these people and how much you owe them in case you have to make arrangements to pay less. See the section on 'Coping with debt' for more details.

4 **Extras** Anything else really. Your luxuries, your treats, your vices and your telephone. Yes folks, the phone is considered a non-essential. Plenty of call boxes you see.

>> p50

Coping with debt

You'll notice that we haven't included any motoring or transport costs in our budget. This is an area you may want to detail separately and have a long hard think about. According to figures published by the government in their 1999 Family Expenditure Survey, on average we spent 15 per cent of our income on motoring costs. By comparison we spent 16 per cent on housing and 3 per cent on our fuel and power bills.

If you are out of work you will have more time to go places, and if you are well served by public transport perhaps you should ask yourself these questions:

● Could I do without a car until I start work again?

● Could I trade in and run a cheaper vehicle?

● How many places I currently go to by car to save time could I walk to or take public transport?

● How many cars are there in my family? Can we manage without one of them?

Having asked those questions and made the decisions, you then have to put transport and motoring costs into the budget. And unless you're disabled any vehicle costs should go into the Extras column.

You may have spotted in the fourth group an item called 'walking around'. This can be a real danger area for those used to having a supply of spending money for the hip pocket or petty purse. And it must be kept tightly under control if you are going to meet the bills and have a bit left over to buy cornflakes.

The problem is that you now have a lot more time to do the actual walking around, and particularly if you live in a town or city, that money can just fly out of your pockets. Many people really have no idea how much they spend each day on this and that. If you're one of those people, try an experiment where you carry a notebook around for a week and detail every single daily purchase you make. You might be surprised. In the course of a day it could look like this for example:

Morning paper 45p

Bar of chocolate 35p

Pack of cigarettes .3.00

Disposable lighter .1.00

Cappuccino 1.50

Danish pastry 99p

Postcard 50p

Stamp 23p

Sandwich 2.00

Magazine 2.00

Scratch card 1.00

Packet of crisps 30p

Can of Coke 50p

Evening paper 30p

Glass of wine 1.99

Fruit machine 3.00

Another glass of wine 1.99

Oh go on then another one 1.99

Kebab 3.00

Cab home 4.00

You've spent £30.09. On what? Nothing much really. It has to come down. Just think about newspapers and magazines for example. On the list above you spent £2.75. If you did that every day for six days you'd be £16.50 a week worse off. That's £858 a year.

Remember, you've got all that precious time to spare now, you can use it differently. As we'll see, access to a broad cross-section of newspapers and magazines is vital to your job hunt. But you don't have to buy them. They're all in the library every day.

Now you've got your budget all neatly written or typed out you need to set about adjusting it. In the first instance you're obviously going to be slashing at the incoming column because the salary figure is going to be seriously reduced.

Next spend a little time looking at the rest of the income and scratch your head about how to increase those figures. Something might jump out at you immediately. If it's possible for someone in the family to work extra hours for example, then convince them to do it if they still want a holiday next year.

If you're stuck, don't worry. Read the section later on about generating new income and let's get stuck into the expenditure.

>> p44

Making money

SAVING MONEY

Short of moving house, and of course practising good energy saving, there is precious little you can do about the first section. Sack the TV by all means, but unless you live alone expect some serious resistance from everyone else.

Be very cautious of the schemes offered by the utility companies whereby you get to pay your gas and electricity on a metered card system. Evidently these work out dearer than buying by any other method.

You could look at changing your supplier: deregulation of the utilities means that pretty much anyone can sell you gas or electricity these days, but do shop around and read some consumer research material to ascertain just who is offering the best deal.

If you are in receipt of benefits or on a very low income then you should apply for Council Tax relief, and of course Housing Benefit if you're living in rented accommodation.

For clothes, food and housekeeping you're in total control. And it can be a lot of fun. Remember you have loads more of that precious commodity, time. You can use it to shop cautiously and you might be surprised at what you achieve. More than likely while you've been working you've been used to going down to the Megamart once a week, piling up a trolley or two, getting the card swiped and forgetting all about it. Quite rightly so. With a hectic work schedule crowding out your life, convenience and speed are the order of the day. But things are different now.

TIP

Put your cards in a bowl of water and freeze them, so you have to defrost them before using them.

You might want to think about shopping every day to make the most of bargains and do it with cash, just taking a set amount each day as set by your budget and seeing what you can buy for that sum. If you do it for less treat yourself to big sticky bun or a bottle of wine. Depending on how much you've saved.

Here's five cool ways to score cheap stuff and not feel like a horrid poor person.

1 **Markets** Pretty much always cheaper for everything. And you get to pick your own out. Obviously you'd be advised to be very careful buying electrical goods, and sometimes clothes can be a little on the nasty side, but for food and household goods a market is unbeatable.

2 **Reduced sections** Here's where you go to the supermarket. You may have to go a few times to find out what time of day they generally go round with their little price gun and start knocking down the stuff that is about to go out of date, but it can be well worth it. And don't worry about food poisoning. A reputable store doesn't sell stuff that's actually out of date, you usually have a day or so to eat it. Look out for stuff that can be frozen for later as well. It's also a good way of trying stuff that you may not have thought about buying previously. Try a trawl of all the supermarkets in your area, just buying things from the reduced section.

3 **Own brands** Come on, you know it's the same cornflakes or beans. They buy them from exactly the same main supplier, spend nothing on branding and advertising and you get them dead cheap. Some places have beans as low as 9p per can, a kilo of flour for 6p or fresh orange for 19p. Try them. And make your family take the blindfold taste test if you encounter any snobbery.

4 **Charity shops** Not just for ancient trousers smelling vaguely of wee. In fact if you go to charity shops in posh areas where people have loads of disposable income you'll be surprised at what they've slung in a bin bag and dumped on Age Concern's doorstep.

5 **Car boot fairs** including flea markets and jumble sales. Again you'd be surprised at what other people consider surplus to requirements. The usual watchword applies on electrical goods, but these are an excellent source of cheap tools, household goods, clothes, books and toys.

Another area of big expense, particularly in the larger family, is the telephone, and while the Consumer Credit Counselling Service people list it in the 'extras' column, most of us consider it a fairly vital part of our lives. Here's another list – the top five telephone-saving tips:

CHANGE YOUR PROVIDER It's fair to say that good old British Telecom ain't the cheapest no more. There's a host of other providers out there offering a range of deals. Most of them make it very easy to switch over, guaranteeing that you can keep your old number and previous facilities. Again, research is the key. Ask your friends which company they use and how happy they are with the service and costs.

USE A FREE TELEPHONE Not as exciting an offer as it sounds. Among the facilities offered by Job Clubs and many training centres for the unemployed are free phone calls, but only in the pursuit of jobs. Still, it takes the pressure off your bill and makes you less conscious of the time you spend on hold listening to the silly tune.

CALL OFF PEAK Calls are significantly cheaper after 6 pm and at weekends, so save as many of your calls as possible until then.

TIP

Auctions are brilliant for buying cheap second-hand and sometimes new furniture.

Obviously if you're calling about jobs then you'll be ringing mainly during office hours.

CALL BAR You can usually get your provider to bar calls to premium line numbers. The exciting world of phone polls, up-to-the-minute sports information and hot 'n' horny chat action will all be denied to you, but the saving will be worth it. Some of those things cost up to a pound a minute and they are designed to keep you on line for as long as they can.

INCOMING CALLS ONLY Probably a bit of a desperate measure but if your bill is becoming unmanageable then it's worth a thought, if only for the length of time that you're out of work.

Saving money on that third group is also quite straightforward, if a little unpalatable. Don't borrow any more money. Chances are you just can't afford it. Get the scissors out and start cutting cards in half. Chuck away all that unsolicited loan application and new credit card junk mail without opening any of it.

MAKING MONEY

Here's your land of opportunity right here and now. What have you always in your heart of hearts wanted to do? What did you want to be when you grew up? What is it that in times of stress and demanding deadlines you always daydreamed about earning a living at?

TIP
Try putting a card in the newsagent's window offering your services: babysitting, bookkeeping, cooking, decorating, gardening, light removals, typing for example.

Tinkering with motorbikes? Gardening? Painting? Give it a go. If you have a desire, a skill and the time to fulfil that dream then it has to be worth a shot for a while. You probably won't make fortunes but you may keep the wheels of domestic commerce turning for a little while. And who knows, it could open up whole new horizons for you. Remember, too, that as we saw in the last chapter there are an astonishing number of training opportunities now open to you: why not exploit them to help you do something you love doing?

Of course if your lifelong desire has always been to be a lion-tamer then realistically it's likely that you'll be hard pushed to find any kind of regular income. So here's another list of five ways you might consider making money:

CAR BOOT FAIRS Yes, them again. You get up at the crack of dawn and you drive some place with loads of other people, and offload everything you don't want/need any more to hordes of avid bargain hunters. Thereby proving Napoleon's assertion that 'The English are a nation of shopkeepers'. Usually you have to pay a small fee to the organiser of the event – sometimes you have to book in advance – and you have to try not to spend more than you make. Be realistic about the prices you charge. Probably best to err on the low side. Given the nature of the customers it's going to be easier to take a pound off a hundred people than a hundred pounds off one person. Scout around the other stalls to see what the going rate for different items is and brace yourself for some bartering.

CRAFT FAIRS/MARKETS Obviously only if you make something or have a good supply of some product. But certainly worth thinking about. Check out 'Farmers' or 'Produce' markets and you'll see people selling all kinds of home-made stuff from chutney and cakes to jewellery and greetings cards. So if you do have a knack for making or growing something you have nothing to lose but your fee to 'stand'.

TIP
Most local councils have a 'Temporary List' of vacancies available in their reception.

EXAM INVIGILATING Obviously this is seasonal work, only really available during exam times, but still worth exploring. Basically you stand in a hall with a bunch of people taking exams. All you have to do is tell them when to start, when to stop and watch that they don't cheat in between time. It's possibly the dullest way to spend three or four hours of your life, but it's reasonably well paid. Ring round local larger colleges about May time to find out how you get on their list. You may need specific qualifications.

MEDICAL TESTING Don't panic. There's minimal risk involved and you're not going to be strapped to a bed while people in white coats drop cosmetics into your eyes. Rumours abound of people having their toes transplanted, hearts stopped and brains removed, but the truth is a lot more prosaic. Drugs companies pay handsomely to put you up in comfortable surroundings for periods of between a couple of days and several weeks. The amount of drugs you are administered is so minuscule as to be practically useless and all you have to do is give periodic blood samples. All the medical testing companies are rigorously controlled by a thing called the Declaration of Helsinki which not only ensures your safety but also insures you into the bargain. You'll also get the most thorough health check-up you've ever had in your life. Check the personal columns in local newspapers, which carry advertisements usually saying 'Volunteers wanted for clinical trials. All expenses paid'. By 'expenses' they generally mean upwards of a hundred pounds a day. Avoid the ones that ask you for money in return for a list of names.

MYSTERY SHOPPING Not always hugely well paid but there are sometimes other perks. It is more or less exactly what it says it is. You pretend to be a customer in a shop or restaurant but you are in fact being paid to ensure that the service and product is up to scratch. You're given a full briefing and usually have to write a report afterwards. A lot of the time it means eating out for nothing. Job Centres and local papers carry ads.

DECLARING INCOME

There's two issues to be dealt with here. For those claiming Job-seeker's Allowance there's the Benefits Agency and for everyone there's the Inland Revenue.

We'll deal with the Benefits Agency first. You are allowed to work while claiming Jobseeker's Allowance without it affecting your overall claim. But it has to be less than 16 hours a week. Although if you're claiming for a partner they can work up to 20 hours a week. Obviously you must tell the Benefits Agency what you've done when you go for your fortnightly signing. When you tell them you've been working they'll give you a form B7 4/98 to fill in. It looks like the one opposite.

You must fill in one form for each job that you do, so if you're working for a temp agency and doing some freelance lion-taming then that's two forms. And when you've declared income once you must fill those forms in every week whether or not you worked. If you didn't do any work for a particular employer you just write 'none' in every available box. If you don't it will hold up payment of your benefit.

Any work that you don't do for an employer, you can declare as self-employed. So under 'employer's details' you write 'self' and put your own address. Remember that your 'earnings' from any self-employed

Declaration of work and earnings

Jobseeker's Allowance

Personal details

Who is working part-time?

Surname

Other names

National Insurance (NI) number

Employer's details in full

Job title

Employer's name and address

Employer's phone number

How often are you or your partner paid?

Pay received

Gross pay (total pay before deductions)
Deductions are the amounts taken off your pay. Please tell us how much was deducted for –

Income tax

National Insurance

Occupational or personal pension

Other deductions –
for example, union subscriptions

Net pay (take home pay)

What date was the pay received?

Pay received was for work done

Was the money for anything other than pay? For example, fares, other work expenses, Working Families Tax Credit.
What was this for?

Hours worked

Dates, hours and minutes worked

What date will the pay be received for this work?

Your declaration

I **understand** that if I give information that is incorrect or incomplete, action may be taken against me.
I **declare** that the information I have given on this form is correct and complete.

B7 03/01

You   You ☐   Your partner ☐

Your partner ☐ Please also fill in your partner's details.

Mr/Mrs/Miss/Ms   Mr/Mrs/Miss/Ms

| Letters | Numbers | Letter | Letters | Numbers | Letter |

Note
If both you and your partner are working or if either of you have more than one job, please complete a separate form B7.

Postcode

Code   Number

Daily ☐   Fortnightly ☐   Monthly ☐
Weekly ☐   4 weekly ☐   Other ☐   How often? _____

Week 1		Week 2	
from / / to / /		from / / to / /	
£	Please attach all payslips for this week. This will help us pay your allowance more quickly.	£	Please attach all payslips for this week. This will help us pay your allowance more quickly.
£		£	
£		£	
£		£	
£	for	£	for
£		£	
/ /		/ /	
from / / to / /		from / / to / /	
No ☐ Yes ☐ Amount £		No ☐ Yes ☐ Amount £	

Week 1	see dates for week 1		Week 2	see dates for week 2	
/ /	hours	minutes	/ /	hours	minutes
/ /	hours	minutes	/ /	hours	minutes
/ /	hours	minutes	/ /	hours	minutes
/ /	hours	minutes	/ /	hours	minutes
/ /	hours	minutes	/ /	hours	minutes
/ /	hours	minutes	/ /	hours	minutes
/ /	hours	minutes	/ /	hours	minutes
/ /			/ /		

Signature

Date   / /

For our use   Date recd   initials | JA095 input – initials   date

---

ILLUSTRATION 4   The Benefits Agency will require you to complete Form B7 if you've been earning work should in reality be your 'profits'. So deduct any expenses you may incur. You may be asked to supply some form of breakdown with your B7. Something along these lines should suffice:

EARNINGS AS SELF-EMPLOYED LION-TAMER

Fee paid	50.00
Less expenses	
Bus fare to circus	2.00
New trousers	20.00
Elastoplast	1.50
TOTAL	23.50
TOTAL EARNINGS	26.50

It's a good idea to keep any bus tickets and receipts – you may be asked to show them at some time. Besides it's good practice in the event that you do eventually sign off and become fully self-employed.

The Benefits Agency allows you to earn up to five pounds a week – ten pounds between you if you're a couple – without it affecting your benefit. After that any wages are cut pound for pound from your benefit on a weekly basis. Although you are allowed to earn as much as you want within your 15 hours and 59 minutes, and your benefit is not stopped until you've actually been paid. Any other benefits and National Insurance credits remain unaffected. Housing Benefit can be a bit tricky. It works more on the basis of how much money you earn, and the Benefits Agency will notify your local authority that you have been working, which will probably entail making a new claim.

And so to the tax collector. You should be aware that your benefits are in fact taxable income. Which means that when you sign off, you will get a P45 to present to your next employer. If you were due any kind of rebate from your last job, you can't have it while you're signing on. Any extra you've paid will be kept back to offset the tax

OFF THE RECORD

If someone reports you for doing a car boot fair, how are my investigators going to prove you made any money? You could say, 'Yes I did it mate but it was a one-off and it was all my own stuff.' To be honest the system doesn't encourage people to declare it, because of the money we claw back off them. Personally I think if someone's going to stand for four hours in the freezing cold on a Sunday morning, and sell off their old junk because they're having a clear-out and they need the money, then that's up to them. Just because they're unemployed doesn't mean they don't have the right to sell their own things. I don't declare it to the Inland Revenue if I do one. But there's no A to Z of rules on this. You're in a very grey area. And it's very much open to individual interpretation by the decision-maker. Which is why you'll get an imbalance of treatment from different staff.

A N Specialist decision-maker at the Benefits Agency

due on your benefits. You'll get the balance when you start work again.

Any work you do for an employer or agency while you're signing on will be taxed. And be prepared to be taxed at the highest rate. The approach that many employers take is that it is best to take a lot off you in the early days and give it back later. If you feel that you're being taxed too highly, particularly over a period of time, then you need to ensure that your local tax office has all your details and that they give your correct tax code to the employer. The tax code is the system the Inland Revenue uses to work out what percentage of your income should be given to them. Your employer should provide a wage slip with every payment detailing those deductions made on behalf of the Inland Revenue. They should also supply a P45 when your period of employment with them ends.

Self-employed income is also of course taxable. This income should be declared via a 'self-assessment' form available from your local tax office. It is your responsibility to notify your tax office that you are operating on a self-employed basis. If you don't it will be construed as tax evasion and you could find yourself in a lot of trouble.

National Insurance contributions are already taken care of: you will be getting credits for the whole time you're claiming benefits.

COPING WITH DEBT

With the best will in the world it can happen. And it's more likely to happen when you're out of work. First off, don't be embarrassed. Chances are it really isn't your fault. And okay, even if you have been a little profligate in the past, that's understandable. We live in a credit-based society where banks and financial institutions are just hurling stuff at you on a daily basis, all designed to get you even deeper in the hole. None of them take the time or trouble to explain just how nasty they can be if you fall on hard times and they decide they want their money back. And look on the bright side, if you've been heavy-handed on the shopping front, you should have a whole load more stuff to sell at the car boot fair.

Remember too that you're not the only one. Everybody is in debt. It's just that when you're working you manage to keep earning just that little bit faster than the interest charges. You stop earning and they start catching up. It's little consolation obviously but even that pillar of society and moral probity, the Queen Mum, has a whacking great overdraft. Just like you, she'd be deep in the doo-doo if she was made redundant from whatever it is she does.

Second thing you have to do, and this is tough, so brace yourself, you've got to confront that beast. Which means opening up all the envelopes, putting the whole lot in a big pile, getting out the calculator and totting up exactly what you owe to whom. Chances are it's going to be a big scary number, but don't panic. You can reduce it, you can deal with it, and if you're smart and get the right help you can stay out of trouble.

help yourself

PLAY FOR TIME. You need it. Don't respond to each letter and demand as soon as it arrives. Wait a couple of days and give some thought to what you're going to say. Any letters you do write, leave 24 hours before you send them so that you're absolutely clear about what you want to say. Then spin proceedings out so that you get maximum time. The first thing to do is query everything. Amounts, dates, interest charges, individual purchases or anything that's written in a jargon that you 'might' find difficult to understand. You never know. An examination of your records and subsequent query may result in having to pay less. Banks in particular are notorious for making mistakes. But you'll also be able to stretch the ultimate payment day a little further. While the correspondence between you and your creditor is 'active', you can't be expected to cough anything up. Particularly if you're questioning something. Send all your responses second class. By the time they've got it, opened it, got to it on the pile, re-examined their records, passed it upstairs, composed a reply, checked it with the supervisor and sent it down to the mail room – chances are you'll have landed a job.

Okay. You made the list? And you looked at the amounts? There's another thing you need to look closely at. Your total monthly interest payments on all bank loans, overdrafts, credit agreements, cards and any other money you've borrowed. That's an overhead. And it's likely to be quite a big one. Go directly to your bank with your figures and the budget you did earlier. Explain the situation and ask if they will consolidate all the debts into one loan, with a manageable monthly payment and a reasonable interest rate that allows you to make some inroads into the debt.

MEANING WHAT?

CREDIT COLLECTION AGENCIES are the companies that banks, building societies and other usurers hire to scare the living daylights out of you in order to retrieve their money. Some organisations use firms of solicitors, but even they pass on debts to collection agencies. They try to recover the amount outstanding, pass it on to the creditor and keep a commission. Sometimes they even buy up job lots of debts for a percentage of their original value. So in the end you may owe only a fraction of your original debt to the collection agency compared to what you owed your credit card company. But you won't know that. The modus operandi is to bombard you with official-looking letters full of scary phrases such as these:

'THIS IS YOUR FINAL WARNING'

'NO FURTHER WARNING OR INTIMATION WILL BE GIVEN'

and the ludicrously ambiguous
'CONDUCT YOURSELF ACCORDINGLY'.

They are just big bullies with hardly any real powers.

51

If the bank gives you no joy then start looking though all that literature you get for and about credit cards. Sooner or later you should spot one that offers you the chance of combining all your cards onto the one, with one monthly payment. Snap it up. And then snap their invidious little piece of plastic in half. It's surprisingly good for the soul.

If you can't find a way to combine your cards cheaply, or your debts are already in the hands of a collection agency, then you're going to have to tackle each creditor individually. At this point you reach for the phone and call up the cavalry. You dial:

FREEPHONE 0800 138 1111

This is the number for the Consumer Credit Counselling Service (CCCS). They are the Debtbusters. Just talking to these guys is going to make you feel a whole lot better. They'll allocate you a case number and a counsellor who will make an appointment to speak to you over the phone and also send you a whole load of really vital information.

The CCCS is a registered charity and its whole purpose is to help out people like us who can't afford to pay our over-enthusiastic creditors. They will advise you and guide you through the various steps required to handle your finances, supplying form letters and a simple explanation of all the procedures.

If it's really bad and you are really scared, they'll even take the whole lot off your hands. They'll administer your finances for you, negotiate with your creditors and ensure that they start receiving some money.

The very first thing the CCCS will want to do is look at your budget, which obviously you've already done. They'll then look at your basic living costs and priority debts and see what's left over for the 'non-priorities'. They'll divide that sum by the number of creditors and make an offer to each one based on that figure. Put simply, if at the end of the month you've got three pounds surplus, and you've got three creditors each owed a thousand pounds, then they'll have to take a pound each. And they'll have to swallow it. It's called a 'token payment' and is based on the principle that you're at least showing willingness and that you will commit to more when you can afford it.

Having made even that commitment though, you must stick to it. Miss even one pound and the nasty letters will start up again.

Now, if things are so bad that you're at the point where you really need the CCCS, then there's a whole heap of questions you want to ask about credit blacklisting, bailiffs, county court summonses and a Pandora's box full of terminology and rotten things. Stop reading this right now and ring:

FREEPHONE 0800 138 1111

They know everything. And everything won't fit into this book. Plus which they are the most qualified people in the world to help.

Whatever the level of your debt the most important thing is to keep a sharp eye on your priorities. Even poor people have to eat. And they need some place to eat in. So ensuring the security of your home is of paramount importance.

If you're a tenant then you shouldn't have too much to worry about. You'll have applied for Housing Benefit and should be getting most, if not all, your rent paid for you. Even if there's been a glitch or you've fallen into arrears, you should be okay. Evicting people, particularly people on benefits, is a long and expensive process. Most landlords are reluctant to go down that road when they know full well that judges are highly unlikely to make someone homeless. So talk to your landlord. Explain what's going on and show them your budget which makes them a top priority. Then come to an arrangement to clear arrears, and again stick to it. The beauty of that arrangement is that there's no interest, so every extra pound you pay is a pound off your actual debt.

A mortgage is a whole other kettle of slimy, sea-dwelling creatures. You've seen all the literature and you know it always says, 'Your home is at risk if you don't keep up repayments.' They mean it. They want the money. And they don't feel sorry for you.

So move fast. The first thing you need to know as soon as you lose your income is how well insured is this mortgage against just such an event? Study that small print closely. Sometimes the word 'insurance' is bandied about in a mortgage document and it refers to insurance that covers the mortgage provider against your misfortune as opposed to you. You still paid for it though. Now you know what kind of sneaky devious people you're up against.

Next thing is to speak to the Benefits Agency. You're unlikely to get much, but you could get some help towards the interest payments.

If your insurance is a no-no then, without panicking them, have a word with your provider about restructuring your payments, perhaps even changing the nature of your mortgage. Remember that you're looking for a short-term fix. You may have chosen the type of mortgage that you did for very sound long-term investment reasons. What you need to do now is cut monthly overheads to the bare bone and not get any deeper into debt at expensive interest rates. Mortgage loans are actually one of the cheaper ways there are to borrow money, especially compared to loans, cards and overdrafts. So just this once, think short-term on your mortgage – you can always return to the long, prudent view when times get better.

TIP

If you work part time and sign on, after three months you become eligible for a 'Back to Work Bonus' when you sign off.

If your provider has you locked into one specific type of mortgage, or will impose stringent penalties for any changes, then start looking at other companies to see if you can remortgage with them. Over the last couple of years there has been a growth in 'flexible mortgages' that allow you to vary the amount you pay off. Some even allow a holiday period where you make no payments at all. If you haven't already got one like that, make a last-ditch attempt to see if you can get one. Obviously if there's little or no income coming into the household then it's likely to be a non-starter, but it's worth a shot. And at this point you still do have a house as collateral.

If none of that works then who you gonna call?

FREEPHONE 0800 138 1111

The CCCS are just as qualified at dealing with your mortgage provider as they are with your credit card company. Let them guide you through the process of dealing with the black hats. One of the things they can do is tell your mortgage people that in future all correspondence on this issue must go directly to them. It may seem like only a small thing, but it does wonders for your peace of mind. It is very distressing to get up every morning to find that amid the now customary mountain of bills is a letter from the bank telling you they're going to take your house off you. You'll be much happier if you never see it. What will happen instead is that the CCCS will contact you, tell you the score in dispassionate lay people's terms and recommend the best course of action.

We admit this is not the cheeriest of chapters. But like the man said, 'Whatever doesn't kill you makes you stronger.' And there is one big bright spot – all that wonderful, invaluable free time you now have at your disposal! Time to read books, watch cricket matches, cook meals, get fit, get fat, learn new skills, catch up with friends, improve your sex life, chuck some bread at the ducks in the park. Whatever it is that you sat and daydreamed about on the way to work. Do it. You may never have that time again. So enjoy yourself.

HOW I GOT THE JOB: *I worked for a mail order company and someone who I worked with, who I'd also known for a long time, left and went to work for the Inland Revenue. She rang me up one day and just said, 'They're looking for casual staff, but with a view to a possible permanent job. If you want to take the chance you could come and work here.' The prospects were significantly better so I went for it, and I got the job because my friend highly recommended me. She was rather highly thought of.*

Trish, revenue officer

The Motley Fool site is outstanding for many reasons, not least because it's well designed and entertainingly written. Even the little messages that come up when a page fails or their service crashes will make you laugh. The site is meant to be a guide to managing your money and investing wisely. They deal with the nitty-gritty of everyday financial problems and debt solutions. One of the most useful parts is the 'The Bribble' section, where ordinary people like you and me send in their experiences and tips for dealing with financial institutions. Highly recommended is a posting from 25 November 1998 entitled 'Here Beginneth The Lesson'. A guy called David Carter has written a brutally honest piece about losing his job and falling into debt which turns inspirational as he claws his way back. The ending, where he turns the tables on his bank, will have you cheering in your seat. The site also carries a huge amount of practical mortgage information.

Simply go to www.fool.co.uk

READ THIS

To be honest we found the books we read on both debt management and alternative sources of income to be pretty dire. They were either extremely patronising ('If you don't have a pen you can buy one from a local stationery shop' kind of thing) or full of vague, wishy-washy advice about 'esteem needs' and 'belongingness'. If that's your bag, head for *Surviving Redundancy* by Laurel Alexander, whose very name fills us with scepticism.

In the mean time, since the subjects under consideration are of such a gruesome nature, may we suggest that you read something light and uplifting to sustain you through a period of great tightness?

If you're stuck for a suggestion, we like the brilliantly funny crime novels by former country and Western frontman of the Texas Jewboys, Kinky Friedman (famous for his minor hit 'If you leave me walk out backwards so I think you're coming in').

NO WAY!

DON'T be ashamed or embarrassed about being in debt. It's not your fault, and you're certainly not the only one

DON'T blow your redundancy money all at once. It's not a lottery win

DON'T put non-priority debts before your eating and housing

DON'T ignore brown envelopes and final demands. Deal with them all in a calm and thoughtful manner

DON'T be afraid of solicitors' letters and nasty missives from collection agencies

WAY TO GO!

DO sit down and explain the situation to family and loved ones

DO make a detailed and explicit budget

DO keep the Benefits Agency and Inland Revenue informed of everything you do

DO cut up and bin your credit/debit and charge cards

DO call the Consumer Credit Counselling Service on 0800 138 1111

GO YOUR OWN WAY

- Consider changing your utilities, phone or mortgage provider

- You might find it cheaper to do without a car or at least restrict its usage

- It seems it's up to your conscience whether or not you declare earnings from certain areas, car boot fairs for example

- You could get your phone service switched to accept incoming calls only

- If your debts are getting you down, you have the option of letting the Consumer Credit Counselling Service administer everything

TEN TASKS TICKED OFF

Explained to my family that times are tough ❏

Prepared my household budget ❏

Got advice on managing my redundancy money ❏

Found reports on cheaper services in library ❏

Organised stuff for car boot fair ❏

Went through all my 'brown envelopes' and dealt with them ❏

Cut up or froze my credit/debit and charge cards ❏

Read through the small print in my mortgage/ tenant's agreement ❏

Called the Consumer Credit Counselling Service on 0800 138 1111 ❏

Made massive gourmet meal from the reduced section. I deserve it ❏

4

VITAL

REQUIREMENTS

* SOUND THINKING

* A BIG PLAN

* LITTLE PLANS

* DAILY SCHEDULE

Plans are nothing, but planning is everything. – Napoleon Bonaparte

Now it's time to get stuck in properly. Time to start the job hunt. Woaoah. Slow down. Put that pen down. Fold that Sits Vac. column up and chill out for a minute. We're going to do this in a nice, easy, relaxed but above all thorough fashion.

You know what they say? Me neither. But there's bound to be some old cliché about an ounce of preparation making haste and spoiling the ship while angels rush in before they leap.

Another cliché that we've all definitely heard is that one that talks about 'competing in an ever-changing job market'. That's right. Competing. In other words, every job that you see and really want, some other person has seen and really wants as well. How are you going to get there before they do? In the first instance by being smarter than they are. P G Wodehouse's creation Bertie Wooster believed his butler Jeeves was smarter than him because he ate a lot of fish. He'd say something like, 'Better crack open another tin of sardines, Jeeves. This looks like a four-fish problem.'

Of course the real advantage Jeeves had was that unlike Bertie, he actually used his brain for solving problems. He had learnt that the muscle between his ears needed exercising just as much as any other in the body if it was to remain effective.

And that's what you'll need to do. Use your head.

SOUND THINKING

We'll check what general shape you're in first of all. How is your head? If you've just lost a job then there's every chance it ain't in too good a shape. If you got the sack because you were persistently sick over the managing director's shoes after a long lunch then it's (a) difficult to feel sympathy for you and (b) easy to see where you went wrong and how to fix it.

If on the other hand you were made redundant or squeezed out by someone younger, cleverer or more closely related to the boss, then that's a tough break and somewhat more difficult to bounce back from. You may well be at a low ebb.

Don't be surprised if you suddenly start to feel bad in ways you never felt before. Under normal circumstances most of us just need a little warning to straighten our heads out. We wake up in the morning feeling grumpy and say, 'What is wrong with me? Too much coffee? Not enough sex? Oh, I know, I'm pissed off because I haven't got a job.' And we make the necessary adjustments. But you may not be operating under normal circumstances. Stress and depression can be very serious illnesses and should be approached with just as much concern as any serious physical injury.

If you do find that 'old black dog' at your heels is turning into a constant and debilitating companion then you must seek professional help. Quickly. Make an appointment with your family GP. Your doctor may not feel fully qualified to help you, but will be best placed to point you in the direction of someone who can give you all the help you need.

There are highly practical implications here for job hunters. People can sense defeat or anger. Even if they can't always identify what's wrong, they'll pick up a bad vibe and plump for the bright-eyed, bushy-tailed, well-adjusted applicant every time. So you have to look after your mental health. And you have to tend and care for your brain over a long period of time. Because it's not just the initial pain of losing your job that can bring problems. The weeks and possibly months that you may have to spend dealing with unanswered letters, negative feedback and lousy interviews can also take their toll.

So how do you keep your spirits up while everything and everyone seems to be conspiring to knock them back down again? Keeping busy should help quite a bit. If you've read this far you'll see that there's lots of things to keep you usefully and purposefully occupied while you're gainfully unemployed. If you read further you'll see that there's a whole lot more to do.

As already mentioned, you might also have to skew your perspective round a little and take a long, hard look at what it is that makes you a valuable person. So they don't want you down at the bakery, despite your unrivalled doughnut-sprinkling skills? Your mum still loves you and believes in you doesn't she?

TIP
Psychologists consider losing your job to be only slightly less stressful than bereavement or divorce.

In fact there's a good way of dealing with the pain of rejection right there. Call up your mum. Have a bit of a moan. She'll soon be telling you how wonderful you are. Of course there's a good chance you already discovered this method for yourself. She'll also give you some advice that we probably wouldn't dare, but might actually be on the money. You know the kind of thing. Eating proper meals. Getting plenty of sleep. Smartening yourself up. Dumping that wholly unsuitable guy/chick.

Those same cliché-mongers we referred to above also reckon that if you ain't failing you ain't trying. And there's something to be said for that. Like Mr Bruce and his famous spider, you're probably going to need several cracks at it before you get a result.

And try not to take every knockback or unanswered letter so damn personally. Obviously they'd soon change their minds if only they knew what a warm and wonderful human being you are. Any employer would have to be insane to turn you down if they were truly aware of how hard you'd work, how much money you'd make them and what a fantastic brew you make. But especially in the early days of sending your CV out and attending interviews you may not always manage to convey those things as effectively as you'd hoped.

This is where you're going to start thinking proactively as opposed to reactively. Think your way into a job, in other words. Use your initiative and start practising some smart-alec behaviour. Eat some fish if you think it will help. We'll do our best throughout the rest of the book to give you some useful tips and practical help, but you're the one who's going to have to develop that mindset which ensures you're more on the case than everyone else who wants that job. And don't think you can't do it. We're all good at solving problems either mentally or practically. We all have skills we can utilise to sort stuff out in our everyday lives, be it solving a crossword puzzle, coping with the kids or putting together a flat-pack wardrobe. Identify your mental skills and deploy them in the job hunt.

LET'S SAY YOU GO for an interview in a large organisation and you suspect it's one of those spurious exercises where someone else has already got the job. Keep your wits about you as you walk around the building and keep your eyes open for a staff noticeboard. In or near the canteen is a likely place to find it. Frequently internal vacancies are posted there before they ever hit the press. On your way out, make a detour, or find some excuse to return that way – you need the loo, or a cup of tea – have a good look at any suitable jobs, and jot down the name and position of the person to respond to. That way you'll be a little bit ahead of the game when it comes to getting your application in. Obviously it would be completely wrong to take it down, put it in your pocket and stroll off with it. Large organisation like that. They probably only have the one copy.

Not only will you get better at finding jobs, but you'll look better to the potential employer as well. They'll be thinking, 'This person showed real initiative and mental clout here. What a valuable asset that could be in this company.'

help yourself

A BIG PLAN

Better make a plan. Actually, better make two plans. One overall, long-term career plan and another supplementary day-to-day plan to get you to wherever the big plan said you should be.

Making plans is a good thing to do because it keeps you motivated and gives you a structure to operate within. A bit like working really. If you master the combined arts of long-term planning and short-term problem solving, then you become a very attractive proposition to an employer. That's exactly what they want – people who think ahead and people who solve problems.

Traditionally, careers advisers recommend making a detailed five-year plan that encompasses three distinct phases. What you want to do now. Where you see yourself in two years. And where you see yourself in five years. You are supposed to monitor and update the plan at periodic intervals.

All of which is well and good provided that in the first instance you do know exactly what it is that you want to do, and in the second instance that it is actually feasible for you to get that job. Supposing you have no idea what it is you want to do. What then?

Well that's where the plan gets a bit trickier, but don't worry, it's all about making lists and asking yourself some questions.

Here's some questions that might help:

LIST NUMBER ONE

- What have I done already that I really like doing?

- What does everyone else say I'm good at?

- What am I trained to do?

- What did I want to do when I was still young enough to have hopes and dreams?

- Do I want to make loads of money?

- Do I want to be in charge?

- Do I want someone else to be in charge?

- Do I want to help people?

- Do I prefer working on my own?

- Would I rather work with lots of people?

- Do I want to work loads of hours?

- Do I just want to work a bit and do something else the rest of the time?

● Who's got a job that I'd really like to do?

● Do I want to use my brain a lot?

● Do I want to use my hands a lot?

Now at this point, many of the other 6,836 books on job hunting available will fill up quite a lot of space with complex charts, points systems and personal achievement/goal fulfilment axis diagrams. We're not going to have any of those. They worry us.

You see, no matter how many charts and diagrams you fill in the fact remains that you are a unique and individual case whose needs and ambitions are yours and yours alone. Sure, you can tick a box that says 'I want a. Money/b. Power/c. Luncheon Vouchers', but no matter how complex the questionnaire it's never really going to work out for you who you really are, and what you really want.

Only you are going to be able to work that out. You may well need to recruit the help of those close to you whose opinions you trust and respect, and maybe even consult a professional to help you focus on what's available. But the last thing you need is to be pigeon-holed into a career choice by some anonymous specialist with an anally retentive take on how people should actually live their lives.

That's not to say you shouldn't give a test or questionnaire a go if you come across one. It might lead you in a direction you never thought of before. It will certainly be food for thought and could give you some great ideas. Just be careful that you don't tick all the boxes, add up all the sums and end up pursuing some entirely unsuitable career as a result. And watch out for those on the internet that encourage you to waste an hour or so filling them in, only to demand $100 if you want to see the results.

So the questions above are intended just as a starting point to get you thinking about what you can do, and more importantly what you would like to do. You have to decide what it specifically is that your career should be, or at least the area you would be best concentrating on.

Of course it's not always that simple. You are also going to have to take into consideration what's available to you. This lion-taming business for example is entirely ludicrous. They don't even have lions in circuses any more for heaven's sake. Get real and snap out of it.

OFF THE RECORD

Nobody really has validated what it is that makes somebody suitable or good at a certain job, so they just take very stereotypical parts of what a job entails and then say, 'Oh, these are the qualities that you need to have,' and then ask people to report on themselves whether they've got those attributes. Some people like to present a self to be recorded that's actually completely different from how they are. A lot of people have really poor insight into how they really are. And all the labels are ambiguous. If you ask somebody if they're fastidious, they'll reply, 'I'm not for some things, but for other things I really am.' It doesn't take into account context and motivation. And there may well be a set of specific skills that are required for a specific job but in fact there are other issues at work. So for example if you're in PR it's not just, 'Do you like meeting people and can you write something?' Very often you've got to have the right voice, look the part and have the networking skills. So you need to be able to research a job in order to present a 'self' that is suitable. But those methodologies that somehow claim to be able to tell you what you would be good at or right for are – I would say – unreliable and invalid.

A N Organisational psychologist

Other factors have to be taken into consideration in the big plan too – your limitations and responsibilities most importantly. You may have to make a separate list of questions that include more negative elements of your personality and circumstances. Perhaps these will help:

LIST NUMBER TWO

● What do I hate doing?

● What have I been criticised for doing badly?

● Am I able to move to the other side of the country?

● Do I have to look after anyone else apart from me?

● What does my partner want from me?

● Is there anything my health prevents me from doing?

● Do my religious or political beliefs prevent me from working anywhere?

When it comes to actually looking at and being offered jobs, it may be worth casting your eye again over the answers to these questions and evaluating how many you may have to compromise and whether or not those concessions are worth making. Everyone knows that in life we have to do things we don't like doing, and most of those things will revolve around work, but the words 'fire' and 'frying pan' might spring to mind. If you have the skills or luxury of being able to hang back a little in order to pick and choose your work environment, then take advantage of them.

Back to the big plan. Did you decide what you wanted to do? You've written 'lion-tamer'. You just don't listen do you? Okay, if your heart's set on it. The next thing to do is write down what it is that a lion-tamer needs to be in order to do their job. Start with personal characteristics, and then move on to the practical aspects. Maybe like this:

LIST NUMBER THREE
- Bravery

- Like lions

- Look good in a top hat

- Training

- Experience

- Contacts in a circus

- A whip

- A chair

- First-aid box

For those of you who chose something a little less obscure than lion-taming this again may be a little trickier. Not always. Some careers are easier than others. I'm a writer for example, so as that's my job it's easiest for me to tell you what I need in order to do it. It would probably look like this:

- Good with words

- Good at research

- Self-motivated

- Enjoy working alone

- A computer

- A good chair
- A big desk
- Reference books
- Contacts in publishing
- Ability to live on fresh air

If I were to make your list for you, then the chances are I would get it wrong or miss something vital out. So you are going to have to do the preliminary research yourself. It's not too difficult. The library should be the first place you go to, then maybe a visit to a careers adviser and finally, but most crucially, again, talk to people who already do that job. There's a twin advantage in this approach, by the way. Not only are you gathering information on your new career but also you're making contacts, or 'networking'. You may even find someone who will be happy to guide you through the processes and procedures, maybe even introduce you to the right people, help you structure and implement your plan. A mentor if you like.

Obviously if you're researching your future career and you find that there is some insurmountable obstacle – can't be a lion-tamer if you're violently allergic to fur – then you're going to have to go back to the drawing board. But generally speaking, if you want it bad enough, there's nothing you can't overcome. A word of caution though. While the plan is important, it's not written in stone. Stay flexible. Who knows what opportunities and openings may pass you by if you stay single-mindedly fixed on the One Big Thing that you first wrote down at the top of this section.

LITTLE PLANS

Having decided on a realistic career and ascertained what exactly you need to achieve that goal, it's time to come up with another plan. This is your strategy for your forthcoming job hunt. Time for another list. This time you want to go back to List Number Three and cross off all those things you know you already have. Then look at the things you're short of and use them as subheadings to make subsidiary lists, along with all other factors to be taken into consideration. A little like this perhaps:

LIST NUMBER FOUR
NEED TRAINING:

- **O-Level Whip Cracking** Class available at local school. Wednesday evenings. Will have to give up pub quiz. Cost: £95. Need to buy whip. Need large space to practise in. Takes a year to complete.

- **Advanced Lion Control** Three-year degree course at University of Bogswiddle. Cost: £2,000. Grants available. Would have to apply in June. Need to move to Bogswiddle. Will need part-time work while there.

You get the picture. If you do that with all the headings and try to legislate for all the implications, you should get a clear idea of how long this thing is going to take and what it's going to cost in terms of money and effort. Once you've got to the level where you can actually do the job you're after, you need to start taking some practical steps.

The first thing you're going to have to do is look at the money situation. Check back to the budget you did in the last section, so you can get the sums as right as possible. Then you need to be asking: how much have you got? How much do you need to live on? And most crucially, how long is it going to last? The most likely answer to that last one is 'not long enough'.

This probably means that you're going to need to have a fall-back plan, a contingency that allows you to earn something while you're looking for the ideal career. For those of us who aren't burglars or members of the aristocracy, that usually means working. The trick here is to try to find work that pays you what you need to live on, but doesn't interfere with the big plan. That could mean exploring some of the casual and part-time options we looked at in the last chapter. It could mean taking part-time or less-well-paid work that isn't too demanding.

If you're unemployed this approach could mean that you are in fact conducting two job searches at once. One to keep the big plan on the boil and the other to find a fall-back job that pays the rent. This isn't so bad. You just need to keep your eye on the ball and keep thinking of ways to progress the big plan. Alternatively you may find that the fall-back job you took to make ends meet isn't that bad

>> p44

Making money

after all. You could happen on something that you really like doing and that also offers you fantastic opportunities to get ahead.

The other consideration you're going to have to take on board is that of time. How long have you got and how long is this going to take? And we're not just talking about hours in the day here, although that's a significant factor, we're talking years to retirement. There's not much point in starting training to be an astronaut if you're 55. You'll be drawing a pension before you get to flight simulation training.

If you've set your sights on the lion-taming job and it takes three years to get trained, but then you can't get a job for three years because there are no vacancies, that's a lot of career path that remains untrodden. I don't know for sure, but I imagine that lion-taming is a young person's game. Lightning reflexes and good upper-body strength seem like they might be desirable qualities. So the more time that passes without you establishing your career the less chance there is of you becoming especially good at it.

What some people do, specifically those in the insecure, creative sectors – actors, musicians, writers, dancers, cabinet ministers – is put a time limit on how long they're going to pursue that path, either in terms of a number of years or when they get to a certain age. In the mean time they develop a back-up career, so that if things do go horribly wrong they're not left high and dry. The spooky thing is that if you talk to people successful in those fields, it's amazing how many just scraped by and then hit the jackpot as they were coming up to the point where they'd promised to quit.

DAILY SCHEDULE

This is really about establishing a daily or weekly regular work pattern and action plan, and then sticking with it. Again, it will reap you double benefits. Not only will it focus your job-seeking endeavours, but also it will be good practice for when you actually land your job. It's another thing employers really like: people who organise their work and then get things done.

Let's assume that by now you've pretty much worked out what you're going to have to do to get your job. You can list it how you like but in essence your basic plan is to buy *Lion Tamer Weekly* and start applying for lion-taming jobs.

You also intend to talk to other lion tamers and ask them how they got to be in the business of taming lions. Maybe you check out any decent accredited courses in your area and see if you can't take one on a part-time basis. Perhaps you write some letters on spec to some respectable circuses and let them know that this is an area you're really interested in and that you are currently studying at an advanced level.

TIP
Keeping a Day Book makes filling in your Benefits Agency Job Search a lot easier.

If you boil that down to its basic constituents, it probably works out at less than an afternoon's work. If that afternoon's work gets you an interview then you've done blindingly well, you're a very lucky person and we'd like to know the secret of your success, because you should probably be writing this book.

The reality is much more likely to be that you're going to be looking for a period of some weeks, possibly even months. Which means that your first attempt is going to fail. And your second, your third and a daunting number of numbers after that. So the first thing you absolutely and definitely need is to get organised. Administration will give you a key advantage over all those half-assed flakes whose idea of a job search is to idly thumb through the paper once a week.

All you need really is a notebook, a ring binder and a pen. That's it. The big secret. The notebook should be big enough to make copious notes and lists in – A4 size is good – and the pen should have a good top for chewing on, I reckon. I call my notebook my day book; you can call yours anything you want.

You write the date at the top of a page and then you make a list of all the things you're going to do that day, including all domestic chores and fun things, and then you tick them off as you do them. I organise mine under different headings:

IN
OUT
BOOK JOBS
WRITE
CALLS AFTER 6PM
EMAILS
WEBSITES

MONDAY 25TH SEPT

DO
SEND ARTS APP.
CREDIT CARD - PAY

BOOK
FINISH C2
BOXES C3 } - SEC 2
INTERVIEWS C3

OUT
JIFF BAGS
PHOTOCOPIES
BANK
VHS

6 PM SIMPSONS

1 PM CALLS
TAX OFFICE - SELF ASS?
STA TRAVEL - FLIGHT
JANNY - VISA QUERIES

6 PM CALLS
HENRY - FLIGHTS
CATHY - TOMORROW
DAD - BEN'S ADDRESS
LUCY - INTERVIEW
PIERS - HOW I GOT GIG?

WEB
E.MAIL BEN
N. WEST FLATURITES
MAIL CAROLINE
WWW. MINDTOOLS.
COM

ILLUSTRATION 5   See how mean I am? Phone calls after 6pm and the internet used off-peak

It tends to look like this page from my day book.

I'm a compulsive list-maker so I even write in the times of any TV shows I want to watch. That's probably a bit tragic, but you decide for yourself. You'll also be appalled by the handwriting, but that's okay because only I need to understand it.

Make a new list every day, transferring the undone tasks to the top of your current list, and of course adding any new tasks that require action. It kind of gives you a feeling of making a fresh start each day and gives your brain time to warm up while you focus on what you have to do.

At the back of the book you can make a contacts/action list. On a separate page for each one, jot down the name and contact details for each person you talked to, what you talked about and what action you took. If you ever find yourself stuck for something to do, go back to it and trawl through to see if there is anyone who might be worth recontacting.

It could look like this:

Fred Stintflone
Redbock Animal Tamers Ltd
12 Craggy Street
Bogswiddle
Tillet
Herts HS1 4JK

Phone: 48409 3033
Fax: 483032 3093
Email: fred@lionsrus.com

Mon 3 Sept. Responded to ad in *Lion Tamer Weekly*

Fri 4 Sept. Filled in application form

Mon 19 Jan. Got rejection letter back

Tues 20 Jan. Wrote and asked if there was any part-time or casual work available

Wed 27 Jan. Phoned to follow up letter

Thurs 6 Feb. Emailed to say I was going to be in the area – is it OK to drop by for chat?

Fri 7 Feb. Secretary called to say Mr Stintflone v. busy. Maybe in a couple of weeks' time

---

TIP
Experts say our brains are better at admin and organisation in the mornings.

You get the picture. But clock this. You're sitting there one day in March flicking through your notes and you see that while you may well have been fobbed off back on 7 February, the secretary definitely said, 'Maybe in a couple of weeks' time,' which gives you the perfect excuse to ring up and say something like, 'Hello, your secretary rang me a couple of weeks ago and asked me call back about this time to arrange an appointment.'

Some people do all of this day book, diary scheduling, task listing, or whatever you want to call it on a computer. In fact most computers even have a special program that allows you to do that very thing. It's up to you. If you feel happier doing it on a machine, go ahead. It's just that personally I find it a whole lot more satisfying drawing a line through a completed task than hitting the delete key.

What you can't do on your computer is maintain your job file. For this you're going to need a good old-fashioned ring binder, hole puncher and some cardboard dividers. Into the folder you are going to put the following sections:

>> p91
Research skills

ADVERTISEMENTS Because if you're applying for a lot of jobs an application form might turn up at some point with no job description and you'll have no idea what the job was. Or at least you may forget something vital. It's also a good way of building up information on which companies are hiring people like you.

CLIPPINGS We'll see in a later chapter the value of trawling though other sections of the press to identify vacancies before they're advertised. This is where you keep your research information.

JOB APPLICATIONS Photocopy each completed application you send in and file it here. That way if you do get an interview you can refer back to it and work out exactly what it was that you said. Make no mistake, the interviewer will have a copy laid out in front of them as they talk to you.

JOB DESCRIPTIONS For the same reasons as above, remind yourself what the job's all about before you go to an interview.

RESPONSES Even the ones that just say 'thanks but no thanks' will carry a name, position and contact details. These could be useful to you if you hear that company might be hiring again.

Once you've put your system in place then you need to set a time aside each day, free from other distractions, when you can beaver away at the job of getting a job. Remember to keep all your files and records updated. Try to get into a routine, maybe even breaking your day book into time slots that dictate when you buy the papers, go to the library, make your calls, write your letters, etc. That way you'll get into a natural working rhythm and when you do start work, fitting back into the work environment won't be such a big deal.

If you've never done anything like this before then you'll also have picked up what the jargon mongers call a 'transferable skill', in other words something you can do in one place – home – that is useful in another place – work. You can confidently claim it as part of your repertoire when applying for jobs. You can say, 'I'm an administrator, me. You should see how I organised my job search.'

HOW I GOT THE JOB: *When I first qualified as a nurse the National Health Service paid for me to go and see a careers consultant and we ended up with this five-year plan to become a community nurse. And that's what I did. But when I actually got to do it I found it wasn't as good as it's cracked up to be and I didn't want to do it any more. So I went for the job I've got now which is junior sister in a group home. I didn't get it because I didn't prepare very well, so I wasn't really anticipating the questions they were likely to ask. And I was quite nervous, I clammed up and gave three-word answers to questions. I asked for feedback after the interview, and what they actually said was that they wondered if I might be too soft when it came to managing staff. But then I didn't give them any reason to think otherwise because I didn't sell myself. So two years later I went for the job again and this time I'd prepared very thoroughly, I'd rehearsed what I was going to say and I'd spent a lot of time thinking about the kinds of questions they were going to ask me.*

Lucy, psychiatric nurse

Real LIFE

Go to www.mindtools.com **and scroll down until you get to the section on 'Stress'. There you'll find a very concise and plain-speaking guide to exactly what stress is, how it affects you, how to spot it and what you can do to alleviate it. We'd recommend**

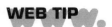

WEB TIP

this site generally as a way of tuning up your thinking processes, but the stress stuff is specifically excellent. It's completely free of jargon and highly practical.

READ THIS

What Color is your Parachute? Richard Nelson Bolles. Ten Speed Press

In the course of researching this book I have read some terrible stuff about jobseeking. Please do have a flick through any book and check it for yourself before buying. Better still, don't buy any. There's loads in the library. That way you can have your intelligence insulted for free. Richard Bolles however is something else. He's an elderly, born-again Christian Yank. Which at face value probably isn't going to motive you to read his book. But it's well worth studying. Accepted, there may be a little bit too much God in it at the back, but you can skip those bits if you're not religiously inclined. The rest of it is a well-written, positive and radical approach to the business of choosing and planning a career, then tracking down the job you've chosen. Be warned, Mr Bolles is not what you would you call conventional. He admits that his approach is 'iconoclastic'. But he does talk a lot of sense and he will make you look at your career prospects in a wholly different way.

NO WAY!

DON'T ever believe that the job you do is what makes you the person you are

DON'T hang around your former workplace with ex-colleagues – it's not healthy

DON'T stop using your brain, you could be in this situation for a while

DON'T be unrealistic about your abilities and obligations

DON'T throw anything away until you've got your job. File all contacts and correspondence

WAY TO GO!

DO take signs of stress or depression seriously and get help

DO get your family to help you through a bad patch

DO keep your problems and troubles in perspective

DO make flexible but detailed career plans, including a fall-back plan

DO organise and administer your job search

GO YOUR OWN WAY!

● If you know exactly what you want to do, make a five-year career plan

● It's up to you whether or not you fill out career tests: just exercise a modicum of caution

● Immediate money problems may mean you have to compromise your main plan for a while

● Devise your own system for administering your job search

TEN TASKS TICKED OFF

Had a long hard think about what I want to do ❏

Discussed it with my family ❏

Listed things I can/can't do and will/won't do ❏

Made a big plan detailing what I want to do ❏

Made a back-up plan, just in case ❏

Made sure that the job I want is in my area ❏

Made my daily planner ❏

Started my job file ❏

Made my contact and action list ❏

Ate fish and chips out of the wrapper with loads of ketchup. I deserve it. And it's good for my brain ❏

5
E S S E N T I A L
THINGS

✳ SPACE

✳ COMPUTER

✳ TELEPHONE ANSWERING SERVICE

✳ LIBRARY CARD

✳ CLOTHES AND APPEARANCE

When you're tall, thin, blonde and have big boobs, you can have any job you want. – Nora Ephron

Looking for a job shouldn't really be a high-overhead activity. Which is a good thing, because you're obviously going to be in maximum scrimping mode. If anyone tells you otherwise then approach them with extreme caution. In fact it's probably best not to approach them at all. Walk firmly away in the opposite direction.

>> p149

Curriculum vitae

We're specifically talking here about anyone who can offer you an expensively produced CV, a top of the range 'psychometric' test or an exclusive careers counselling service for a fat fee up front. As we saw in the last chapter, testing can be an arbitrary and unreliable process. We'll be showing you how simple it is to produce a top-notch CV for a couple of pence later on.

MEANING WHAT?

Psychometric does not mean a nutter with a tape measure. It's a nutter with a list of questions. The dictionary says psychometrics is 'the science of measuring mental capacities and processes'. The application of that science in job hunting is through testing processes that are supposed to ascertain whether or not you have suitable skills for certain types of work. It goes a little beyond testing your numeracy and literacy and we'll be dealing with it in a little more detail towards the end of this chapter.

>> p86

Essential things

Careers counselling services should be looked at as closely as any other service you have to pay for. If you really feel you need some one-on-one advice, then don't just pick the first service that hoves into view. Do your consumer research. Ask if you can talk to satisfied clients and trust your instinct. The one that works when you choose a solicitor or plumber. And remember that there is a whole heap of free advice out there for people in your situation. Your local Job Centre will have rafts of information on what's available in your area.

Bear in mind that you may not have too much money, but you do have that priceless commodity – time. You can use it to research and discover pretty much anything about any career all by yourself.

There are a couple of things you'd be advised to dig deep and fork out for though. We've listed them below, although the first one won't cost you anything extra.

SPACE

You need some. Just to sit in, put your stuff down and make sure it's there when you come to pick it up again. We're talking about a mini-office really, if you can manage such a thing. Just a flat surface, with a chair, preferably near the phone with all the other accoutrements of your new job-hunting profession to hand.

ILLUSTRATION 6   At **www.onlinepsych.com** you can do your own psychometric tests

Ideally you should be closeted away from the TV, noisy children and any other domestic distractions. In reality you're probably going to have to enlist everyone's cooperation to ensure they understand that for a set time each day you're going to be working at getting work and will need some peace and quiet.

The best possible scenario is that you sit there for that set period and work like a Trojan at the task of getting your job.

COMPUTER

We realise it may not be the best time to be thinking about a big capital outlay here – although if you got a redundancy payment, it might be worth a look – so think about blagging one. All you need is access to it for a few hours a week. But you do need one. They make the writing of letters and the production of your CV so much easier both to do and to keep track of.

As we'll see in the chapter on CVs, you may have to change yours pretty frequently. Once you've got it onto a computer, it's a couple of minutes' work to rewrite whole swathes. A good computer will also give you warning of any spelling mistokes (this one's no good) and if you haven't used one before, you'll be amazed at how good you can make a document look. Besides, it just looks so professional. No matter how neat your handwriting may be, or how smart you are at typing, nowadays everyone expects, or at least prefers, to see things laid out in the crisp, clean lines of a modern word-processing program.

>> p149

Curriculum vitae

Here's a few options you could try for a freebie. All you need is a supply of floppy disks so that you can save the work you do on any machine and return to modify it later:

YOUR LOCAL LIBRARY Most have some sort of computing section nowadays. Rates are quite cheap, often reduced or even free for the unemployed.

THE JOB CLUB OR RESOURCE TRAINING CENTRE They're not going to let you play games or write your memoirs, but for the everyday business of writing your CV, and sending out letters, that's exactly what they're there for.

A FRIEND Loads of people have got computers at home now. Maybe in return for doing something they haven't got the time to do – cooking them a nice meal perhaps, or a bit of weeding – you've got an accommodating buddy who'll give you reasonable access to their machine.

A SEEMINGLY BENEVOLENT INTERNET PROVIDER It's not really taken off in the UK yet, but it probably will – in the States a number of companies have launched schemes whereby you get a free computer if you sign up to their internet service. If this happens to you, be very wary. Check closely if you are liable for monthly charges and whether or not you're free to terminate the service without penalties. The main catch is that the company will want a full consumer profile from you so that they can direct an advertising campaign specifically at you, via your computer.

If you have no experience of computers and are nervous about using them, then now is your chance to get up to speed. While there are still a lot of jobs out there where you don't need to be

OFF THE RECORD

The computers are set up to display advertising any time they're used, not just when you're connected to the internet. And you get a hell of a lot of it on your screen, so obviously the plan is to bombard you with products until you buy some of them. But it occurs to me that if you can't afford to buy a computer and get online, to the extent that you sign a long-term deal for a free one, you're unlikely to be doing much spending. I don't think the companies have thought this through. I bet when the figures come in for how much the advertisers have actually recouped through this medium, the offers will be withdrawn pretty damn quick.

A N Computer salesperson

computer-literate, businesses and organisations are relying on them increasingly. Getting clued up can only be advantageous to improving your job prospects. Training is available in abundance. Local colleges, libraries, skill centres and voluntary organisations all have simple step-by-step courses running throughout the year. And computers are dead easy to use. Honest. The Luddite technophobe who wrote this book managed to do it all on a computer, so there's hope for anyone. If you can drive a car, play a fruit machine, or make your microwave work, you can very quickly get the hang of banging out letters that look like they were produced by Miss Moneypenny in her prime.

TIP

When buying a computer, check the 'helpline' isn't a premium rate number. Advice could cost more than the machine.

If you do feel that you've got money to buy one, then we trust you're sussed enough to shop around, do some research and consult a couple of experts. One word of warning though. While using computers is simple enough, setting up and getting one started can be a different prospect. They're not like a vacuum cleaner. You can't just plug them in and start work. Make sure that you've got reliable help in person, or at the end of a phone, to guide you through the more difficult bits.

It's impossible these days to talk about computers without mentioning the phenomena of the internet and the World Wide Web. And there are practical jobseeking implications that need to be addressed within that sphere. We'll be addressing them later on.

TELEPHONE ANSWERING SERVICE

>> p41

Saving money

We're assuming that you've got the actual telephone. Also that you've read the previous chapter about minimising the cost. What we're about to suggest may mean a small outlay, but it will be worth the expense.

The point is to ensure that potential employers can always get hold of you. They are likely to be very busy people and probably quite keen to get their vacancy filled. If they call you, and get no reply, then there's every chance that they won't call back again. Particularly if they're ringing around for a number of candidates to attend interviews and they fill that quota with people they got through to the first time.

There's two ways to go here. Your phone service provider will usually have a feature that can be installed directly onto your phone line, the cost of which is added to your regular bill. You can choose between having an anonymous, disembodied voice that takes calls when you're not available, or personalising your greeting. The feature is usually available for quite a small fee and in the event that you don't need it any more, it should be relatively simple to have removed.

TIP
Get your hands on as many phone directories as possible. It's still free to access information from them.

The second way to go is to buy one. They do come reasonably cheap and if you go to one of those modern high-street pawnbroker-style shops such as 'Cash Converter', you'll get a decent second-hand one with a six-month guarantee. Ensure that whatever you buy, the instruction book is enclosed. Some of them can be quite tricky to operate and it's not a bargain if it turns out to be useless.

It's up to you whether or not you have a mobile phone in order to make you even more accessible. It might be worth it if you're intending to be out a lot, but the chances are you're going to be at home. Bear in mind that a lot of organisations issue guidelines to employees instructing them to call someone on their mobile only if it's urgent. It's unlikely that calling you to arrange an interview is going to fall into that 'urgent' category.

And of course you know that no matter how the mobile phone companies have jazzed up their deals, they are always significantly more expensive to use than land lines. Plus, if you're still in belt-tightening mode, can you really afford to have two phones?

help yourself

IT'S NOT WIDELY publicised for obvious reasons, but a Directory Enquiries call to British Telecom will cost you – at the time of writing – 40p! That's nearly a fiver to get hold of a dozen numbers. However, if that's the only way you can get hold of a number then call from a payphone. Up until October 2000 it was free, but BT now charges 20p a call. Still not cheap, but half the price of calling from home. By making a list of all the numbers you require, waiting until you're passing a call box and doing them all at once, one after the other, you could save a small fortune.

LIBRARY CARD

You'll have noticed that we've mentioned the library a lot. And we're going to mention it a lot more. If you're not used to hanging out in the library, you might just think of it as a place where you borrow books. But the modern ones can do a whole lot more than that for you. Especially if you're looking for a job.

They all take a wide selection of newspapers and magazines, including specialist trade rags carrying loads of vacancies.

The reference section will carry all sorts of useful stuff, from leaflets with the very latest advice on benefits, education, job-creation schemes and volunteering to lists of local companies.

Many now have new technology sections with good CD-ROM sections, access to computers – all fully webbed up – and training sessions to help you get going.

Basic stuff

IT LOOKS LIKE A CD and it works like a CD, except that it's got loads of ROM on it. ROM stands for 'read-only memory' and means that instead of having tunes from the latest chart-topping beat combo on it, it's got staggering amounts of information. To give you an idea, an entire ten-year archive from a broadsheet newspaper will fit onto just one disc. You merely pop it into the little tray in the front of your computer and the whole lot is available to read. See all those snappy little quotes at the top of the chapters? I got them off a CD-ROM that seems to document just about everything that anyone ever said about anything.

Librarians are also highly trained to extract the relevant information from any medium at high speed, so exploit that facility.

CLOTHES & APPEARANCE

Unless of course you're qualified to work in a nudist camp, you're going to need some decent threads. And you're unlikely to want to be splashing out in some high-fashion boutique on the latest haute couture creations.

So look after the best suit you've got. Make sure it's dry-cleaned and in good repair, then bag it up, mothball it and save it for the express purpose of going to job interviews.

Sorry guys, but for practically all interviews a shirt, tie and smart shoes are pretty much de rigueur even today. Obviously if you're going for a job in a bank or insurance company you would kind of expect that level of conformity, but even in less austere occupations you should really make the effort. It gives out a signal of being prepared to make an effort and many interviewers feel it shows them a degree of respect.

One absolute no-no is an 'amusing' tie emblazoned with popular cartoon characters. It sends out a whole host of negative signals, not least being that you are so lacking in any sense of style or humour that you have been forced to try to buy some from a multinational company. And believe it or not there are still middle-aged, middle-management, middle-brow types out there who will see even that small gesture as akin to joining an environmental action group in order to fire-bomb financial institutions. Yes, we know your kids bought it for good luck. Put it on and leave the house in it. Have the real tie in your pocket. Just don't forget to swap them back before you get home.

For women, it's pretty much the same deal, except you can forget the tie. Go for a smart shoes and smart suit in something fairly neutral. Keep the heels low and the neckline high. You know what we're trying to say here. And we know that there's a school of thought that says you should go to an interview dressed to knock 'em dead. But it's better to be safe than sorry. Suppose the person interviewing you is a woman? Or a gay bloke? Or a sensible personnel officer with a large male staff who would like them to keep their minds totally on the task in hand?

Shoes are important here, folks. Sturdy, shiny and sensible. God knows why, but evidently research reveals that people do look at

TIP
Second-hand shops are brilliant for decent ties. Just ensure there's no soup stains down the front.

footwear as a test of character. Remember that you may be walking about a bit as well, both to and from interviews and perhaps also if you're given a guided tour of the premises. Bear in mind that Sod's law dictates that it will rain on your big day. So keep a cloth handy to wipe them over before you go in. Or, here's a handy hint, go to the interview in your trainers/wellies/Jesus sandals but with your posh shoes in a bag, and then simply change them before you get there.

And don't worry about getting all ponced up in your nine-to-five glory only to arrive at the interview to find everyone lounging around in Lycra and fishnets. They understand that you're putting on a style for a purpose and you can always stress the point if they're looking at you as if you're some 'sort of like, weird suit guy, man'.

Before we close this chapter we'll do a list here of all the things we have gleaned from the experts about appearance and personal grooming at interviews. It's up to you how you dress and adorn yourself at all times, but let's hope you recognise that compromise is sometimes necessary in order to reach your goal. You know *we* don't want to patronise you, but:

 DON'T let your hair obscure your eyes. You need to be able to make eye contact. It looks like you're hiding behind it.

DON'T have a hairstyle that means you have to keep messing with it. It's distracting to the interviewer.

DON'T forget to shave. Stubble is trouble. Looks great on George Clooney. Looks like you haven't bothered to shave.

DON'T have spectacles patched up with wire, sticky-tape and matchsticks. Looks like you're not bothered about details. Make sure they're clean as well.

DON'T wear shades. Dark glasses render it impossible to make eye contact.

DON'T wear too many dark clothes. It looks too gloomy. So have some discreet colour splashed about. Trainee undertakers or hitmen can ignore this advice.

DON'T wear garish socks. Not just for interviews, but in life generally we would've thought.

DON'T wear jeans, and no trainers, no baseball caps, no sportswear. Come on, you'd do it to get into a fancy nightclub.

Brightly coloured hair is a no-no.

DO clean your teeth. And check in a mirror before you go in. Just in case bits of breakfast are hanging around between your teeth.

DO use some breath freshener or gum before you go in. But don't keep the gum in for the interview. Don't take it out and stick it behind your ear either.

DO keep those nails clean and short and tidy. It's another weird thing people look at as a test of character.

DO remember it will rain. So a raincoat, a hat and/or umbrella are all worth considering.

DO carry a bag. But not a plastic carrier bag from Cheapo Supastores. The recommendation is a small attaché case or leather folder. Don't have two bags if you're a woman. Put everything into one smart, slimline affair.

DO leave all your other accoutrements, spare shoes, umbrella, coat, ski-mask in reception before you go into the interview. You don't want to be fumbling around with stuff while you're in there.

DO make sure you look okay from the back as well. You don't want the skirt tucked into the knickers thing happening do you?

DO watch out for the translucent. You don't want the knickers showing through the skirt thing happening do you? Trainee clip-joint hostesses can ignore this advice.

DO wear a bra. And tights or stockings. No, fellas, you can definitely ignore that.

DO ditch any badges, jewellery or insignia that affiliates you with any kind of religious, political or social group. You might just arouse some prejudice in an interviewer. Particularly horrible one that isn't it?

DO have a hanky. In case you've got a cold, hayfever or allergies to slimy bigots. Tissues are not good. They get too snotty too quickly.

DO have a bath. And use deodorant. Oh for crying out loud. Honestly, that's one of the top ten tips in the opinion of a lot of 'recruitment experts'.

Big dangly earrings are off the agenda. So is jewellery that rattles. Unless you're after Jimmy Savile's job. Whatever that is.

Guys? Lose the jewellery altogether.

All those guides and manuals that go on and on about the 'ever changing workplace' seem to have forgotten that one of the things that changes is people's attitudes to style and dress. If you wanted a job in a skateboard shop for example then you'd be well advised to pierce everything that protrudes and cultivate some really radical/ludicrous facial hair.

If you are genuinely concerned about what you should wear for an interview then a sensible move might be to visit the company in advance, if at all possible. Hang around outside as people are leaving or arriving and clock what the majority of them are wearing. That way you can get a measure of what's acceptable in that specific workplace.

HOW I GOT THE JOB: *I didn't feel particularly inclined to invest in a suit, but I did borrow a tie. My girlfriend said, 'You should take your earring out', which I did. I thought no one bothered about stuff like that, so when I went for the second interview I left it in. Not to make any statement, but just because it's part of me and I never think about it. They said, 'There's a dress code. Do you mind wearing the corporate colours, T-shirt with a logo on, etc.?' Which I didn't really mind. And then it was, 'Do you mind not wearing your earring?' I said, 'No, not at all,' and I didn't wear it for the first couple of months. But the guy who interviewed me said that it was the big boss who didn't like it. When I finally met the big boss, he was a really sweet guy, and he had an earring in. I think my immediate boss is something of a fascist. Now I wear it all the time. I know it annoys him, but they daren't sack me for it. Besides, I'm the best goddamn printer they ever had in their lives.*

Gary, printshop manager

While psychometric testing is becoming increasingly prevalent in recruitment selection, few of us get a chance to see an actual test until we go for an interview and are told to 'fill this out'. As in any kind of testing, the trick is to know what kind of method you need to be able to succeed. However, if you're looking for help on the internet, you won't find it a whole lot of use. There are plenty of descriptions and quite a bit of debate going on, but not too many actual test examples. The fact that there's a lot of people asking for money to provide sample tests and results may give you a clue as to why. However we found some useful sample tests with instant evaluation at the most unexpected site. **www.majon.com** is a marketing and PR firm for website companies. When you get there look at the 'Extra Resources' menu and click on 'IQ Test Selection'. Not only will you find loads of useful stuff about different kinds of selection tests, but there's some that you can actually take and get instant results for.

READ THIS

Understanding Psychometric Testing in a Week. Gareth Lewis and Gene Crozier. Hodder and Stoughton

Conversely, there seem to be hundreds of books available that give you an opportunity to practise and understand psychometric tests. They're all pretty much of a muchness, but this is one of the clearest and, even more attractively, one of the cheapest at £6.99.

NO WAY!

DON'T give your money away. Be sceptical of 'professional' services to help the unemployed

DON'T expect a new computer to behave. You will have some teething problems

DON'T wear a tie with a cartoon character on it

DON'T go for a job interview dressed to break hearts. It could backfire

DON'T be smelly at an interview

WAY TO GO!

DO make sure you've got a quiet space dedicated to your daily job hunt

DO get computer literate

DO get hold of all the phone directories you can lay your hands on

DO go to the library. A lot

DO think in advance about how you're going to look at interviews

GO YOUR OWN WAY!

- If you can't find a free careers counsellor and think you need to pay one, that's fine. Just be sure to shop around

- If you're offered a free computer, that's great, just check the small print very closely

- You can buy a telephone answering machine or get your phone company to provide a message service

- Use your best judgement to decide exactly how to dress for your interview.

TEN TASKS TICKED OFF

Allocated some space for my job hunting ❏

Been to the stationers ❏

Found out about taking computer lessons ❏

Called my telephone company to ask about a message service ❏

Called at the post office and got up-to-date directories ❏

Joined the library ❏

Got my best clobber dry cleaned ❏

Went and got a decent haircut ❏

Found a tie in the Oxfam shop ❏

Asked the most attractive librarian out for a coffee. I deserve it ❏

6
V I T A L
SKILLS

* RESEARCH SKILLS
   * NETWORKING SKILLS
     * TELEPHONE SKILLS

The wind and the waves are always on the side of the ablest navigators.
– Edward Gibbon

This bit is all about being ahead of the game. How you can get to that job a little bit faster than some other guy who doesn't deserve or need it as much as you do. Make no mistake, there are jobs out there. There are always jobs out there. Think about it. How many people today must have retired, got promoted, moved jobs, got fired, won the lottery, or died? They all left vacancies behind. Those vacancies must be filled. And you have as much chance of filling them as anyone else. But you do need to be a little better and a little faster off mark than the other guy.

So you may need to polish up in some of the following areas, and like we keep saying, it cuts two ways. Any good work you do in order to get the work makes you look good to a prospective employer. Take a look at the list of skills covered in this chapter. Are they not attractive qualities to have in an employee?

We're not saying that you'll read this chapter and immediately become the most competent researcher who ever phoned a contact and clinched a big deal at the very next meeting. That would be misleading. These skills are like any others: you have a certain amount of natural aptitude to help you get started, you pick up some handy hints, and then the rest is a case of practice making perfect.

We're here to supply the handy hints and get you started. And the first thing you're going to need to know is where the jobs actually are. 'In the paper, or the Job Centre,' you might be thinking. And you'd be right. But they must have existed for some time *before* they appeared in the paper or anywhere else. By the time they're on public display, anyone can see them. What you need to do is try to get at them first.

RESEARCH SKILLS

Research is just a case of finding stuff out. We all do it all the time. If you've ever done DIY, cooked, bought anything, found out when your favourite TV show is on, then you've had to do some research. All you have to do now is angle that research towards job hunting. And it's another of those lovely two-edged benefit thingies. What is one of the things employers really like? People who can efficiently find stuff out on their own initiative.

Actually, this one really holds a triple-edged benefit, because if you do manage to get an interview, the more you know about the company you want to work for, the more impressive it will look.

The main part of researching anything is keeping your eyes open. Information about your specialist subject – in this case job hunting – is all around you. As a researcher you just have to become attuned to somehow plucking it out of the air. Take a look at this hypothetical daily routine and see how many bits of useful information might come your way.

8.30 AM:

The radio alarm clock goes off. You hear the news on your local radio station. 500 new jobs are to be created by Megacorp Ltd when they open their new factory in September.

8.45 AM:

You pick up the mail. Among the junk there's a leaflet declaring 'Special Opening Offer!!!!! Carpet Warehouse!!!!! Massive Reductions!!!!! Hurry. Etc.!!!!!'

9.00 AM:

You catch the regional TV news. 'And in financial news Corpameg Ltd announced that they made a pre-tax profit last year of 41 zillion pounds.' And there's an interview with a man in a suit saying that the market had responded very favourably to their new wonder widget, with sales outstripping supply for most of the year.

9.15 AM:

You nip out for a bottle of milk. On the way you pass a building site and look at the signboard that says 'Coming Soon. A New Shopping Experience from Cheapo Supastores.'

9.45 AM:

You eventually get out of the shop with your pint of milk. It took ages. There was a huge queue and the solitary shop assistant was clearly unable to cope.

9.50 AM:

A dirty great big articulated lorry pulls up alongside you and the driver asks for directions in broken English to what sounds like 'Porcamag Ltd'. You've never heard of it, but it's on Mount Street so you're able to point him in the right direction.

You get the picture? You've just spotted six potential new job openings and you haven't even had your breakfast yet. Let alone opened the local paper. And when you do settle down to your tea and toast over the *Bogswiddle Recorder* you'll probably find another half-dozen *unadvertised* jobs.

TIP
Check to see if the company you're researching has its own website.

The financial and business pages will carry items about mergers, takeovers, expansions, senior appointments and new clients. The advertisements will tell you of new stores, businesses, restaurants and services that are coming soon, or have just recently opened. The small ads will tell you who is applying to open new licensed premises, what buildings are having their usage changed and which planning applications the council is looking at. By 10 am you've got dozens of potential jobs to explore. And we hope you're not making the mistake of thinking that any of those enterprises are limited to one field when it comes to job prospects. Just because Corpameg makes wonder widgets it doesn't mean that they only want skilled widget wibblers. They'll also need accounts people, legal experts, administrators, caterers, maintenance staff, receptionists, drivers and people with all manner of skills. Some of which are bound to be in your area of expertise.

Having gathered your basic research material, you need to expand it a little. Find out who these people are, what they do, what they're like to work for, how much they pay and how to get a job from them.

THAT'S RIGHT, FOLKS. I don't even really have to say it now, do I? You need to go the library. Then it all becomes so easy. The reference section is packed with directories and reports on every company in the world. Literally. From huge great giants like the Disney Corporation and ICI down to your local pub, you can find a book or CD-ROM which will tell you everything you need to know.

Basic stuff

If you're not used to using a reference library, show your list of companies to a librarian and explain exactly what it is you want to do. They'll give you a lesson in how to find stuff out and in no time you'll be whizzing round the shelves like a professional. Don't forget either that the libraries carry extensive numbers of periodicals, not just newspapers but a lot of magazines specific to certain professions and trades. These are jam-packed with insider information and contact details.

Finally you call the company up, tell them you are doing a research project on local firms and ask if they have any literature they can send you. Ninety-nine times out of a hundred, they're only too happy to send you reams of stuff about how wonderful they are. Occasionally you'll be questioned a little more closely. 'What do you want it for?' they'll say suspiciously. Possibly because they're concerned that you're a competitor trying to snoop on them, but perhaps because they have something to hide. You can be as honest as you want. 'I'm considering a change in career and wanted to look at everything that's available before making a decision' is fine. Or you could pretend to be a student researching local economic trends in widgetery if you want to remain incognito.

Now you've got just about all the information that it is possible to get in the public domain, which is great but still not enough. What you need now is stuff the public doesn't know about. Specifically, what jobs are coming up and how to get them, but also whether or not you'd really want to work there. All well and good spotting a high-rolling job at a profitable company in a field that you've always wanted to work in. But suppose the person you'll be working for is a neo-fascist with halitosis, and everyone else in the company has got green lungs because the widget wibbler gives off noxious gases.

What you need is the inside dope. You could also do with finding an ally within the company who can let you know what the score is, maybe even put in a good word for you if you decide you want to work there. You need to get to know some people. You need to brush up your networking skills.

NETWORKING SKILLS

Networking just means talking to people. That's it. Talk to a lot of people and you're networking well. Again, it's something we all do. If you've ever organised a party, played any team sports or passed a birthday card round the pub for everyone to sign, then you've done some networking.

If you're networking to get a job you don't even necessarily have to talk to any scary strangers in the first instance. Talk to your family and friends before you do anything else.

Make a list of everyone you know and start ringing them up or going to see them. Ask them some questions. What you basically want is the answer 'yes' to one of the following questions:

- Do you work at Corpameg?

- Do you know anyone who works at Corpameg?

If you got a 'yes' to the first one then you're laughing. And you're asking another bunch of questions:

- What's it like to work there?

- Do you know if there are any jobs going?

- What kind of people are they looking for?

- Do you think I could do that job?

- Would you keep your ears open and let me know if you hear anything?

- Who does the actual hiring ?

What you never do – unless you're talking to your Uncle Rupert and your surname's Murdoch – is say, 'Can you get me a job there?' Because the chances are they can't and that will just be embarrassing for you both. What they can do – and will probably be pleased to do – is act as an intelligence service, point you in the right direction and tip you off if they hear of anything.

This is sometimes sneeringly referred to as 'nepotism'. You'll hear embittered and failed jobseekers moaning, 'It's not what you know, it's who you know,' as if that was some kind of criminal offence. Let's be straight about this. In the first instance your Uncle Bert would have to be insane to recommend you to his boss for a job that he knew you couldn't do. If that were the case he'd either be honest with you, telling you he didn't think you were cut out for the job, or he'd fob you off with some excuse as to why he couldn't speak to the boss.

TIP
Allocate some time each week specifically for the purpose of networking.

MEANING WHAT?

Nepotism means giving favoured status to someone you're related to. It comes from the Latin word for 'nephew' and refers to the practices of certain popes who would hand out special favours to their nephews. Turns out that much of the time these so-called nephews were in fact their illegitimate sons. Presumably that's the origin of the expression 'some other bastard got the job before I'd even applied'.

In the second instance, think of it from the employer's point of view. If you had to pick someone to work with day in day out, sometimes under pressure, wouldn't you rather work with someone you knew? Or at least someone who someone you knew told you about. Especially in small and medium-sized companies, advertising a vacancy through the press is the very last resort. The boss will much prefer to use personal contacts to fill a position. It's cheaper and it's safer. The boss gets someone with a personal guarantee of good faith from an employee who daren't jeopardise their position by feeding the boss dodgy information. All you have to do is become someone the boss knows, or at least has heard about.

In the third instance, think of it from your point of view. You need and want that job. I'd like to meet the person who found themselves in the above position and said, 'I couldn't possibly attend that interview because Uncle Bert recommended me. Morally it would be just wrong.' You'll be as good at that job as anyone else, otherwise Uncle Bert wouldn't have stuck his neck out. He might quite like going for a pint with you but he isn't going to sacrifice his career for a deadbeat is he?

Of course it might not pan out with Uncle Bert. He may even tip you off that Corpameg is not all it's cracked up to be and you'd be better off out of it. So don't stop there. Approach all your uncles and aunts and nephews and nieces. Then start in on your friends. Practically every single person you know must work some place. If you know only 20 people, and you're talking to them all, that's 20 places that you may know of a job coming up before anyone else does.

If you've specifically targeted Corpameg as the place you want to work but you don't personally know anyone there, then you need to fall back on asking everyone you know question number 2.

● Do you know anyone who works at Corpameg?

Eventually something like this should happen:

UNCLE BERT:
Yes I do, feller by the name of Fred, used to be on my morris dancing team, lives off Mount Street. I go for a drink with him every Wednesday in the Duck and Drake.

YOU:
Any chance I could tag along with you on Wednesday? I've always fancied working there, I want to ask him what it's like.

UNCLE BERT:
No problem. I'll introduce you to him.

Now you've really networked. You've made a contact – through someone else – who might be able to get you even closer to whoever does the hiring at Corpameg. You must treat this contact with all due care and respect. Don't waste it and certainly don't abuse it. When you meet Fred, make your intentions clear and ask as many questions as you can think of, but don't ask him for a job. In the first instance he probably won't be able to give you one, and in the second instance, unlike Uncle Bert, he doesn't know you from Adam. Treat the exercise initially as a fact-finding mission and secondly as a way to get to know Fred better. If you are genuinely keen to work at Corpameg, he'll spot that enthusiasm, and it will make an impression on him. Let's hope that next time a vacancy comes up he'll remember you and put in a word, or tip you off via Uncle Bert.

Of course he might walk out and forget all about you, or he may decide that he can't stand the sight of you and you'll never hear from him again. It doesn't actually matter, because now you should be getting into the swing of this networking thing. You'll be asking all of the 20 people you know, 'Do you know anyone who works at Corpameg?' and you'll be introduced eventually to someone else who might be able to help you. Besides which, if you've been smart, you'll have gleaned all sorts of useful information from Fred just by asking the right questions and listening carefully. Questions like:

- What's the boss like?

- Who's in charge of hiring people?

- What kind of people are they looking for?

- Here's what I'm good at, do you think they'd ever hire someone like me?

- What would be the chances of coming down and having a look around the place some time?

If you stick with your networking you should eventually find yourself in there talking to the right person. If that's because they've heard about you and invited you in for an interview then hooray! Skip the whole of the next section, go straight to the bit about interviews and get your suit dry-cleaned.

If it's because you've managed to engineer a meeting or introduction through one of your contacts, then at some point you will feel that it is the right time to ask about any vacancies. Make absolutely sure, before you do so, that you are talking to the right person. And be honest. Maybe along these lines:

YOU:
I've been dying to meet you. I've always wanted to work at Corpameg, I just love widgets to bits, and you guys are the best widget wibblers I ever met. Would you let me know if anything came up that I might be suitable for?

If the person who hires people is sussed, they'll recognise some key things about you after they've talked to you for a while:

- You administered your job search.

- You researched their company.

- You networked resourcefully.

Sometimes it may not be possible to find someone who works – or knows someone who works – in the company you've targeted. Or perhaps you need to act fast on the information you've gleaned from your research. What then?

One option is to just stroll in, march up to the first person you see, probably a receptionist if it's a biggish place, and do it like this:

YOU:
Can you tell me who's in charge of hiring please?

PERSON:
Yes certainly, it's Ernie Sludge.

YOU:
I wonder if it would be possible to have a quick chat with him. I just have one quick question – it'll only take 30 seconds.

If you do it that way you've got around the standard receptionist line of 'He's very busy. Could you call and make an appointment?' Also when she – it's almost always a she – goes to ask him, or rings him, she'll be able to stress that you're not going to take long.

Nine times out of ten the guy will come out and see you. He may have left specific instructions that no one can see him, but the truth of it is that people get very bored sitting in their office all day seeing the same old faces, and a bit of a walk down to reception breaks the routine a little.

When he gets there, you must stick to your word. You said 30 seconds, and you promised just one question. Only if he insists must you stay any longer. What you should do is have a little pitch prepared. Not just prepared but rehearsed out loud and timed beforehand. It could go something like this:

YOU:
Mr Sludge, thank you for coming out to see me. I've just dropped by because I know you're one of the best widget wibblers in the business, and I just got my Third Dan Wibbling Belt, so I'm looking for opportunities at the moment and wondered, if you did have any positions here, how I would go about applying for them.

What's he going to say? 'I'm sorry, but we don't employ enthusiastic, resourceful, trained wibblers here. In fact we're hoping that the whole company grinds to a halt so that we never have to recruit anyone ever again.' Not likely. Even if he's got nothing specific for you, and who knows, he might have, he's more likely to say one of the following:

● 'We normally advertise in *Widget Weekly*.'

● 'We've nothing at the moment, but if you'd like to leave a copy of your CV we'll put it on file.'

● 'Leave your name and address and we'll contact you if anything comes up.'

● 'Why don't you make an appointment to come and have a chat with me next week some time?'

Whichever one it is, you've got your foot in the door. You've made another contact. Make sure you've got his name and number – perhaps he'll give you a card – and use them wisely. For example, if he gives the first response, you can jog his memory when you apply for the job, maybe like this:

> Dear Mr Sludge,
>
> You may remember I called to see you a few weeks ago and asked about the position you have advertised. . . .

To walk up to the front door of a strange place and start asking to see people can take some chutzpah, but that's a useful and employable skill to develop. It's understandable that if you've never done anything like it before you may find it daunting. But it's worth a shot, and you'll find like anything else that the more you do it the easier it gets. If you're really nervous you could take a friend along the first couple of times for moral support.

help yourself

IF YOU'RE WORRIED about going into a company that you really want to work for and blowing it through nerves, then practise on companies that you have no real interest in working for. You can polish up your pitch and networking skills on a whole host of dull and uninteresting jobs, and you might hit on something unexpected. The same goes for the using the phone bit. Practise on some abattoirs and fast-food joints.

If you feel that just marching up to the door is a bit much, then there are other things you could try. Where do people from Corpameg go at lunch times and after work, for example? Possibly a perfect excuse to hang around bars in the interest of research!

Another place to do great networking is at conferences, exhibitions and trade fairs. You'll find details in the specialist trade magazines, and if you can get along to any, the benefits in terms of not only contacts but also insider information will be immense.

The thing you must remember is to be nice to everyone. You never know where people might crop up again, or in what way they could be useful to you.

That receptionist of Mr Sludge's for example, she might be promoted to personnel officer next week. Even if she isn't, there's every chance that she could have input into your future, even if it's only Mr Sludge saying, 'What did you think of him then?' Which is bad news if you've just been snotty with her.

The one big drawback with networking in the ways described here, by talking to people, visiting them, cold-calling, is that it is time-consuming. It could also get to be expensive if your horizons go beyond your local town. You can't just drop into Corpameg in Ashford, Kent if you live in Ashton, Lancashire for example. That's where you're going to have to use the telephone.

OFF THE RECORD

Sometimes people underestimate you because you're the receptionist. They think, 'Oh, what does she know?' But I know loads, all the mail, calls and information pass through me. And I'm very short on patience: if someone calls and they're being rude to me, I'm just rude right back. Or if someone comes in and they're making my life difficult because they can't get to see someone, they'll not be taken very seriously at all.

A N Receptionist

TELEPHONE SKILLS

We all probably take the phone for granted. All our lives we've had access to one and conducted all our personal business, family affairs and much of our love lives over it. But this is a different ball game. We need to be aware that we are about to be dealing with very busy people who use the phone in their working lives as a tool to get things done. And if it's true that first impressions count the most, then we also need to be aware that we may not get much time to make a good one.

>> p81

Telephone answering service

Give some consideration to the answering of calls. We hope you've taken note of the last chapter and invested in some kind of answering service, but you've still got to consider how the phone is answered when you're in. And by whom.

Some people think it's cute to let their small children answer the phone, and if their grandma's ringing, it probably is. But if you're expecting a call from the humourless and impatient chief executive of Corpameg Ltd, you'd be ill-advised to leave him to negotiate with an over-excited three-year-old. Same goes for teenagers who have just discovered – and believe they invented – the hysterically funny joke of taking calls in a peculiar voice while claiming to be from some fictitious establishment.

TIP

Where does the pen by the phone disappear to? Make sure yours is tied down if necessary.

You yourself should really be answering the phone for the duration of your job search, particularly between the hours of 9 and 5 when you might be expecting the most important calls. If that's not always possible then try to inculcate the rest of the household into some of the good telephone practices herein. And make sure they understand the importance of taking full and detailed messages which give you the name of the caller, the time they called, their number and any message. Stationers actually sell little notepads as pre-printed forms with spaces for all those details.

Unless you have one of those gadgets that tells you who the incoming call is from, then you have no idea what's going to happen when the phone rings. So brace yourself. Don't answer it on the first ring, take a moment to compose yourself, imagine it's the very important man from Corpameg, sit down and focus your mind. Homer Simpson always says 'Yello' (as incidentally does Bart) and look at his career prospects, so that's probably a bad way to answer. Some people reel off their telephone number. Which seems

TELEPHONE MESSAGE FOR _____

IN YOUR ABSENCE A CALL WAS RECEIVED

FROM _____ TIME _____

ACTION

MESSAGE
TAKEN BY _____ DATE _____

ILLUSTRATION 7   A inexpensive message pad like this is well worth getting

a little pointless. The caller just used the same number, they don't need confirmation of the fact. Perhaps the best way to go is to state your name very clearly, like this:

'Hello, Kevin Smith speaking.'

Aside from anything else it saves time and trouble of the 'Who am I speaking to?' sort. The caller knows immediately if they've got the right person. Then all you have to do is sit and listen, with your pen poised. The experts recommend having a mirror in front of you so that you can check that you're smiling while you talk. Apparently, the smile somehow transmits itself to your voice and squeezes down the telephone lines to make you sound like a happy little elf.

After that you're pretty much on your own. No one can predict how the call will go, but the key has to be in the listening, focusing tightly without any distractions on exactly what you are being told, and trying also to learn something about the type of person you're dealing with.

When you make calls you're much more in control. First, you can plan before you even pick up the receiver. If you're not used to making lots of calls and you're worried about how you might sound, then try making tape recordings of calls that don't matter too much. Play them back and listen to how you did. Look out for the following:

SPEECH WHISKERS So there you go. Whatever. Okey dokey. And so forth. Blah de blah. Y'know? I put those in because they're little verbal tics that some of the people I speak to regularly use throughout their telephone conversations. In some cases they're downright annoying; certainly they can have the effect of making you pay less attention to what they're actually saying as you start to focus – perhaps even subconsciously – on their vocal idiosyncrasies.

HEAVY BREATHING Some people just breathe louder than others. You must have had someone ring you up and sound as if they're panting with lust when they're just trying to arrange a meeting for Tuesday. It's easily fixed, you just hold the mouthpiece a little further away from your mouth.

HESITATION Umm, err, ahh, weeeell. You know the kind of thing. If you take a call from someone like that, you find yourself silently screaming, 'Get to the bloody point.'

WITTERING Might not be a real word that. But it means going on and on about nothing particularly relevant, for no reason and at great length. How do these people afford their phone bills? It's probably the worst faux pas you can commit when talking to someone who's offering you a job, or interview. In the first instance they're too busy to listen to you rabbiting on about nothing, and in the second, they'll be thinking, 'If I employ this person they're going to spend hours talking on the phone instead of working.'

Having paid some attention to the way you generally speak on the phone, you next need to get down to some specifics. Here's the deal. You've got a big list of people to call and on that list is Ernie Sludge, chief personnel officer at Corpameg. First thing to do is think about when to do it. Generally speaking Monday morning and Friday afternoon are bad times to try to speak to busy people. Friday afternoon because they're trying to get everything signed off before the weekend, and Monday morning because they're dealing with all the stuff they didn't get squared away on Friday.

Lunch times can be a good time to try if you're finding someone really hard to get hold of. Very busy people often eat lunch at their desks. Another tip for finding busy people at their desks is to call before 9 am or after 6 pm when everyone else has gone home. If they are workaholic, they'll be in at all hours. You also stand more chance of getting directly through without having to deal with a third party. More of which later.

Next you need to have a bit of a think about what you're going to say. Some people recommend making a little script and reading it out. It's up to you, but since you've been at home a lot you must have taken a load of calls from people selling you stuff, who you just know are reading from a script. And it annoys you doesn't it? You try to throw them off the script because you know they're about as interested in you as you are in their double glazing.

A better way to go might be to jot down two or three key words and perhaps a couple of questions that you need to get answered. By all means have a little out-loud rehearsal, but you should be wary of giving Mr Sludge the impression that he's just one more name on a long list that you have to get through.

When you pick up the phone and dial, one of three things happens:

● You get a third party in the shape of a secretary, personal assistant or receptionist.

● You get an answering machine.

● You get the person you called.

Sorry folks, but the last one is the least likely. So we'll deal with it first. You've got your key points and questions, you've done a little rehearsal and you've practised making phone calls on people who don't matter. You'll be fine. Just introduce yourself, stress that you won't keep him long (keep that promise), and launch into your spiel, which might be something like this:

YOU:
Mr Sludge, my name is Kevin Smith and I'll not keep you a minute. I'm a fully qualified widget wibbler and I understand that from time to time you have vacancies at Corpameg. I wondered how I might go about applying for any that are coming up in the future?

>> p94
Networking skills

The rest you know because we covered it in the last section. Just listen to the guy, and keep jotting down what he tells you – he may be giving you another contact name and number, or details of a specific job. When he comes to the end, and you've found out all you need to know, thank him for his time, hang up and add the details to your contact list. Like all the other stuff in this section, you'll get better at it the more you do it.

If you get an answering machine or voice-mail service when you call, then hang up immediately. Have a quick rethink. You were psyched up to speak to a person, you see, but a machine is a different entity altogether, requiring an entirely different approach.

The less information you leave on an answering service the better. Mr Sludge has enough on his plate without listening to an interminable message from you which incorporates your full career details including hobbies, interests and marital status. The bare facts will do. They should include the following:

YOU:
Hello, Mr Sludge.

His name, just in case someone else picks up his messages.

YOU:
Kevin Smith here.

So he knows who you are, obviously. But also switching from one name to the other creates a feeling that you maybe know each other. He speaks to a lot of people, so there's no reason why he shouldn't believe he does know you. 'You don't know me but . . .' for similar reasons is probably not good.

YOU:
Bert Smith suggested I give you a call.

Obviously only if he did. This is where your contacts come into play.

YOU:
I'd appreciate it if you could give me a call.

Just being polite.

YOU:
My number is . . .

Slowly and clearly. Include the dialling code.

> **YOU:**
> **That's . . .**

Repeat your number, just in case he had to scrabble for a pen.

And that's all you need to say. Everything else is superfluous. You don't want to be tying up his tape with details that you'd be better placed to put over in person, and mentioning that you're looking for work might slide you down his priority list. Don't expect a rapid response. You may have to go at it a couple of times. Don't be a pain in the ass, either: if there's a message from you every day, he's going to expect you to be telling him something that is vital to him – you could rub him up the wrong way.

The most likely thing that's going to happen when you call is that you get some third party, possibly one who is under strict instructions not to let you speak to the person you need. The great American comic Lenny Bruce had a theory as to why so much television and pop music is mediocre. He figured that truly talented people are of a sensitive and insecure nature, so they find the prospect of having to deal with fierce secretaries and receptionists too daunting. They try to get hold of the person who has the power to hire them, but are quickly deterred by what Bruce called a 'militant attitude'.

The second-rate writer or performer on the other hand, the one with what Bruce referred to as 'moxie' and 'stick-to-it-ness', would be persistent, he'd find a way to get around the third party to ensure that his stuff was seen and heard. If you recognise yourself there, then you don't need me to tell you how to get around the third party, but if not, then here's a couple of helpful suggestions.

Obviously not all third party staff are deliberately obstreperous and unhelpful, but they are likely to be busy and under pressure, which is why you don't want to make life any more difficult for them. Remember that if you trick them in some way into letting you speak to the boss, then they could get into trouble. Again, rule number one is to be polite but to combine that with gentle persistence.

Bear in mind too that anyone else you speak to in that company is potentially a contact and therefore someone who might be helpful to you in reaching your objective.

Suppose you ring, then, and this happens:

YOU:

Hello, could I speak to Mr Sludge please?

THIRD PARTY:

May I ask what it's in connection with?

Don't lie. That's just going to cause you and the third party a whole load of trouble and get Mr Sludge's gander up into the bargain. On the other hand there's a good chance that the third party has a pat answer for everyone who might be ringing up to ask for a job. The pat answer might serve you well, so maybe the first time you let them give it to you. And if they sound like a friendly person, perhaps they can answer some questions for you, and be of some help. If you know you don't want the pat answer, then you have to think of something else to get you through or get your call returned. Here's some possible suggestions:

● 'Bert Smith suggested I give him a call about widget wibbling.'

● 'I have some questions that I'd quite like to put him to personally if that's at all possible.'

● 'I was wondering if it would be possible to make an appointment to come in and see him regarding career opportunities for qualified wibblers.'

● 'I've just qualified as a wibbler and I was told that Mr Sludge was the right person to talk to give me some advice on a technical matter.'

You'll probably develop stratagems of your own, but those above should all get you beyond the 'Put your CV in the post. Click. Brrrrrrr' response that is familiar to many jobseekers.

If it gets you straight through to Mr Sludge then well done, make a note of the ruse you used and try it again on the next call. More likely it's just going to get you further into a dialogue with the third party. Once you're two or three sentences in you could try making a friend of this person, crack a small joke, or say something like, 'It's just started pouring down here. Is it raining there?' That great British icebreaker, the weather, gets them every time. Get their name at the very least, and don't forget to write it down in your contacts book.

You most likely will have to call back, and the chances are you'll get the same person you got the last time. You know this person now, and they are beginning to know a little about you. So work hard at becoming their friend, and try to get a little information out of them each time you have your little chat. Maybe something like this:

> YOU:
>
> Hello. Can I speak to Mr Sludge please?
>
> THIRD PARTY:
>
> I'm sorry, Mr Sludge is in a meeting, can I help?
>
> YOU:
>
> Oh hello, it's Arbuthnot isn't it? Kevin Smith here, I called last week, how are you today?
>
> ARBUTHNOT:
>
> I'm fine thanks. Can I help you at all?
>
> YOU:
>
> No, that's okay, I was just trying to get hold of Mr Sludge. Busy man, isn't he? If you were me, when would you figure would be a good time to call?
>
> ARBUTHNOT:
>
> Well, I'm not sure. He is very busy, we've got a lot on at the moment.
>
> YOU:
>
> Really, well that's good news isn't it? I was reading the other day that a lot of widget wibblers are going through a quiet period.

You get the picture. Don't keep Arbuthnot hanging around if he sounds like he's also very busy, but each time you call, try to get that little bit more from him. Eventually you could find yourself chatting like old friends, and maybe now you can recruit his help.

> YOU:
>
> I don't know, Arbuthnot, this is the fourth time I've called and still not heard anything. Do you reckon I'm barking up the wrong tree?

If you're nice and chummy with Arbuthnot he will start to feel a little responsibility towards you, he will mention you to Mr Sludge

– 'That Kevin Smith rang again, he seems like a really nice guy.' You will also become locked into Mr Sludge's list of people to call, and he'll just do it. Because your number is there and he does do stuff. When he finally does so, it is politic to make no reference whatsoever to the trouble you had trying to get hold of him. It sounds as if you're trying to score a point, and could make him defensive to the point of not liking you.

Reading the above won't make you an instant expert in researching, networking and communicating but you should have picked up a few tricks of the trade. The rest is down to practice and instinctive thinking as you develop your skills. Once again, you will be practising things that make you an even more desirable employee.

HOW I GOT THE JOB: *I've done a lot of temporary work for the local council, and I picked up one of their temporary job lists – which anybody can do – saw the job in there and thought 'I can do that'. I'd worked in a library years ago. I applied for it, and did an interview. They sent a letter saying that I was suitable but they didn't have any space for me. Then eight months later they re-contacted me and offered me the job. I think I got it because I'm good with people, I like working with the public. I got that across at the interview by being open and honest and not putting on any airs or anything. Some people think they have to pretend to be something they're not, but I'm not like that. I made the odd pathetic joke. Unless they're really dour, people usually like that. I wasn't over-enthusiastic, because that can be a pain, but I tried to be really interested.*

Claire, library assistant

READ THIS
Dun and Bradstreet Business Register

This is a huge book, or rather a huge series of books. You can't afford to buy it at £119 per volume, but your reference library should carry it. Basically it's a listing of every single company in the world, and to make it easier for you they've put each region into separate volumes, so the one that covers your area can be carried to a desk without the aid of heavy lifting machinery. It's updated yearly and it will tell you how long a company has been established, the company structure, the nature of its business – indexed for specific reference – how many employees there are and the all-important contact details. It even gives you a rough idea of how much a company is worth, and how likely it is to go bust!

Here's a site that's useful and funny to look at into the bargain. Go to www.users.bigpond.com.fmcdonald/index. There you will find a picture of an Australian geezer who looks exactly like Rolf Harris in a dodgy wig. He claims that he's really a psychologist called Frank McDonald, and he's got a pretty well-designed site with a range of clearly written articles on a number of useful topics. For the purposes of this chapter, check out his advice on improving your conversational skills, which bizarrely he's also translated into something he calls 'jive speak'. For future reference he also has good bits on managing worry, depression, and maintaining mental health at work.

NO WAY

DON'T just go asking your friends and relatives if they can get you the job. Most times they can't and it could lead to embarrassment

DON'T ever take up more of anyone's time than you promised

DON'T let just anyone answer your phone any old how during office hours

DON'T leave long-winded messages on a potential employer's answering service

DON'T lie to a third party about why you are trying to speak to their boss

WAY TO GO!

DO keep your eyes peeled all the time for unadvertised job vacancies

DO go to the library. Again. And again

DO see if the company you're interested in has a website

DO use your friends and relatives to help you make contacts

DO be polite and friendly with everyone you meet. Who knows how they may be able to help you?

GO YOUR OWN WAY!

- Cold-calling on a company can be a useful way to make contacts and find vacancies

- You could practise your networking and phone skills on companies that you'd never want to work for

- You might be able to make contacts by hanging around bars and cafés where the staff go for lunch

- Visiting exhibitions, conferences and trade fairs can be an invaluable source of contacts

- If you're worried about how you sound on the phone, record yourself, listen and adapt accordingly

TEN TASKS TICKED OFF

Been to the library and checked out the research resources
   on local companies ❏

Asked everyone I know for a hiring contact at their
   workplace ❏

Made a list of companies I'd like to call on ❏

Moved the phone to a convenient position and
   nailed a pen to it ❏

Explained to the family that I must take all calls during
   the day ❏

Made a tape recording of one of my phone calls ❏

Made a list of the companies I need to phone ❏

Rehearsed what I'm going to say when I get through to
   the right person ❏

Made notes of everything that was said and to whom in
   my contacts book ❏

Rang my best buddy and talked complete nonsense
   for an hour. I deserve it ❏

7

LOOK

* PRINT MEDIA

* THE VOLUNTEER BUREAU

* AGENCIES

* THE INTERNET

A man willing to work, and unable to find work, is perhaps the saddest sight that fortune's inequality exhibits under the sun. – Thomas Carlyle

While researching, cold-calling and writing unsolicited letters are undoubtedly the most effective ways of discovering unadvertised vacancies, you will of course need to know about some other places to look.

Mainly because those methods are clearly very time-consuming and don't allow you to get a broad overview of all the opportunities available. Plus you ideally need to be advancing on all fronts when it comes to attacking this here 'ever increasingly competitive job market'. The more irons you have in the fire, the more likely you are to get a result.

PRINT MEDIA

This is where everybody looks for a job. Even people who have perfectly good ones with massive salaries and desks the size of Norway are not averse to casting their eye over the 'Situations Vacant' section of the paper. Which means that competition for those jobs listed in the paper is the fiercest. This is where the rat race well and truly starts.

The first thing you have to do is understand the nature of the beast. You need to know how to suss out what the job ads actually mean. Not difficult in most cases, but there are some tricks of the trade you might like to watch out for. What we can't help you with is the highly specific and frequently esoteric jargon that accompanies the copy for particular trades or professions: you'll have to research that for yourself. But in general there are clues in there to what the company is like and what they're looking for. The first clues are in where the ad is and what it looks like. A simple line saying 'Lion-Tamer Wanted. Call Billy 485738 309302' in the *Bogswiddle Gazette* tells you that you are dealing with a small outfit with a limited budget, but also quite an informal and friendly set-up. The contact is listed as 'Billy' as opposed to 'Mr Smart' or the 'personnel officer'.

Proper old-fashioned established companies with secure jobs are probably the easiest to spot. They'll be boxed and presented well enough to be noticed, but not overly conspicuous. The contact person will usually include their title and the name of the department along with a precise job specification and clear application instructions. The same goes for government and official bodies. Their ads will carry the logo of the organisation and frequently a little strap-line telling you exactly what they do. 'Bogswiddle Metropolitan Borough Council. Dedicated to Bringing the Best Services to the Local Community' for example.

A fancy display box with a flashy logo and lots of cleverly written copy tells you that someone is trying to make an impression. That could be because they're doing really well, and they're keen to attract the best staff available, or they might just be showing off to their clients and competitors. Hoping that they'll clock the ad and think, 'Blimey! Look at the kind of people they can afford to employ.' These kind of ads sometimes carry a list of skills and qualifications that would deter a genius. Paradoxically that can make them worth taking a shot at. It might mean that the employers are setting their sights too high and ultimately may have to settle for someone a little less perfect. A nifty thing to do is keep an eye open for repeat ads. If you see a job and think, 'That sounds fantastic, but there's no way they'd have me,' keep your eye on the paper you found it in. If it appears again in a week or two, you know they've failed to fill the vacancy. That's probably because they're asking the impossible for the money they're offering, and they might reconsider their recruiting policy. Just be aware that it could also be because everyone who works in that business knows that they're a bunch of fly-by-night cowboys who won't last until the next payroll's due to be delivered.

OCCASIONALLY YOU'LL SEE a job advertised in a newspaper inviting applicants to reply to a PO Box number. Who are these people and what do they have to hide? Those two questions put a lot of job hunters off, justifiably. They could be a gang of dodgy con merchants, sleazy porn-brokers or, even worse, MI5 looking for spies. If the ad specifies the profession – advertising, showbusiness and the financial sector are common – then it could be that an employer is advertising incognito either to test the loyalty of its own staff, or to try to find out who is disaffected enough to rat out on their competitors. But the PO Box number is not always as anonymous as people like to think. If you call the Post Office's Sales Advisory Service (number in the phone book) they'll happily give you the address of the company to whom the box belongs. They won't give you the name, or a telephone number, and they can't supply information on private boxes. But you're a research animal and an address is all you need. If it's the same as the one at the top of your payslip, then probably best not to bother applying.

help yourself

CODED PHRASES

In all cases you need to familiarise yourself with some of the verbiage inherent to some job advertisers. Like estate agents they've developed a little code that they think the rest of us are too dumb to crack. The following list is by no means definitive but it will give you an idea. It would also be unfair to suggest that any employer who uses some or all of these phrases is trying to mislead you. Some of them will just be jargon junkies. Here's some of the things an employer might 'require' from a worker:

SELF-STARTER Either you'll be the only one in the office doing any actual work while everyone else goes to 'meetings', or the job is in telesales, probably on a low basic wage with commission provided you work like a dog.

GOOD ORGANISATIONAL SKILLS You'll be doing a lot of filing. 'Well organised and efficient' is a variation on the theme.

ENTHUSIASM MORE IMPORTANT THAN EXPERIENCE They can't get anyone from within their own industry or profession to work there at any price. And the price is probably low. Usually preceded by the words 'Hectic/Frantic/Busy City Centre (insert glamorous business title here) requires assistant to the producer/director/editor/etc.'

SENSE OF HUMOUR You'll probably need it every time you open your pay packet. But it could also mean that they're downright weird. Perhaps working in a field that your elderly aunt may not entirely understand, or approve of. Oddly, this one can often mean working in clothing that most of us would find very unfunny. Possibly no clothing at all.

LOW BOREDOM THRESHOLD Means exactly the opposite of what it says. The job is so mind-numbingly dull that you will start to find paper clips fascinating after you've been there for about half an hour.

ABLE TO WORK ON OWN INITIATIVE They're going to put you in a little room, all on your own and make you stay there until you've done everyone else's work.

ENJOYS A CHALLENGE The challenge of trying to remember what your house looks like. You'll be working all hours of the day and some kept back for emergencies. Pay specific attention to the wages on this one. In fairness, a lot of employers who expect to own your soul will pay handsomely for that right.

GOOD PEOPLE SKILLS Most likely you'll be in customer complaints or on a consumer helpline. This is a major growth area and there are a lot of good companies with excellent work practices, but be advised that there are also some real stinkers. If you decide to ask a current employee how they find it, don't do so over the phone. 'All calls may be monitored for training purposes.'

TIP
There's a list and links for all UK magazines and newspapers at www.ukbusinessnet.com.

DO YOU WANT TO BE RICH? Translates as 'So do we. That's why we're running ads like this and scamming suckers like you.' Please don't fall for this, or any variation of it, no matter how impressive the literature, sales presentation, video, training day or row of Porsches outside the premises. Obviously you realise that if anyone offers you a job in return for which you give them some money, then it's not really a job. But there are other more subtle ways to set you up. Some of them are so obvious you could laugh, but some are so cunning and sophisticated you could end up crying. Watch out for 'pyramid selling' scams under another name and remember, if it looks too good to be true, it probably is.

MEANING WHAT?

Pyramid selling is where someone – sometimes called a sponsor – gives you, or more likely sells you, a 'starter kit' or 'system' for a product or service which you then sell to other people. Every time you sell something you make a small profit and your sponsor makes money too. A percentage is also made by their sponsor, and so forth back up the 'pyramid'. You don't actually make much money from the sale. What you're supposed to do is recruit the person you sold it to, sell them a 'starter kit' or 'system' and encourage them to go out and recruit everyone they know. Every time you recruit someone you get a commission not only from their sales, but also from the sales of all their recruits, and of course you pass a percentage back to the person who recruited you who passes it on to the person who recruited them. The people at the top of this pyramid make a big pile of money. The ones at the bottom – the majority – make peanuts. That's a simplified version. The companies who devise these schemes are often very sophisticated operators using the darker sides of modern sales and motivational techniques to con you something rotten. In its purest form pyramid selling is actually illegal in the UK, so look out for 'Network Selling', 'Multi-Level Marketing' and anything else that offers you a millionaire lifestyle for the price of a video, a ticket to a 'conference' and a big box of dodgy old tat.

OFF THE RECORD

The chain of people above you is called your 'upline' and the ones below you the 'downline'. The punter never actually pays commission to the upline. It's usually done by the company computer. Depending on your 'level' or 'status' you buy either from the company or from your upline at a fixed retail discount, wholesale if you've got your own downline. Once you 'qualify' – usually by buying a container load to fill your garage with diet powder you'll never manage to sell, or by convincing a number of other mugs to sign up and do the same – you also get a monthly royalty or bonus payment from the company. The ethos is based solely on the ability to play on people's greed, but we dress it up a little so they'll feel better about themselves. We say, 'If I could show you a way to increase your family's financial security and help a bunch of your dearest friends, you'd be interested, wouldn't you?' That's the 'affirmative close', always delivered nodding. Fact is, it's the best way I know how of losing all your dearest friends 'cos you're round there every other day harassing them to buy ersatz designer perfume.

A N Multi-level marketing director

SALARY DETAILS

The other area where confusion and chaos can reign in the world of job advertising is in the details given about salaries. Sometimes they're not even given. If there's no reference to money whatsoever it either means there ain't a great lot, or that the company is so huge and prestigious they don't need to start quibbling about the odd couple of grand here and there for the right applicant. The style of advertisement is going to tell you which one you're dealing with. In most cases there's a figure listed and that's it. If you can't live off it, don't bother applying.

Government and official bodies usually list salaries like this: '£12,000–£15,000'. The lower figure is the least you could ever be paid. It's known as the 'entry-level salary'. They usually make it quite clear that the actual sum is dependent on age, experience and qualifications. The higher figure is the most you could ever expect to get paid in that specific job. Each organisation will have its own policy for working out the exact figure, and they may be willing to explain it to you over the phone or at the interview.

Here's a rundown of some of those codes that deal with the cash. Again, it's not foolproof, some companies won't even think about the message they're giving out when they write their copy. But if you put it together with some of the other clues in the ad, it should give you a rough idea of where they're at:

CIRCA Could mean that they're just playing it safe, hoping the right person comes along and doesn't want too much money. Usually it means that the salary is negotiable. But it can also be a circuitous way of saying, 'That's all there is, chum.'

PACKAGE WORTH Means that the figure they quote is not what you're going to get in hard cash. It could include a whole host of variables from free car parking to company stock options. It's not hard to see which you're up against if you look at the ad. If it's the one liner 'Lion-Tamer Wanted. Salary Package Worth £20,000,' you can figure that a chunk of that is going to be in free circus passes and a tab at the burger stand. If it's a big display ad, you could be looking at health cover, pension plan, company car, subsidised canteen, free health club membership or a whole host of things. Most reputable companies will outline the benefits in their job specification details.

SALARY NEGOTIABLE Means they haven't a clue what they can pay, perhaps even who they can pay. Usually used by a small company that hasn't had much hiring experience. Don't be put off. It may mean that you can seize the initiative and help thrash out a way of ensuring that you reap the benefit for all your hard work and consummate skills.

OTE – OVERTIME EXCEPTED The basic wage may not be too high, but the company has options for people who want to boost their salary by working longer hours or shifts. The rate per hour should be significantly higher for those periods, but the supply can be unpredictable. Also means 'on target earnings', meaning that if you don't make your sales target, you won't be paid anything like this figure.

BASIC in big letters followed by 'with bonus and commission' in smaller ones just means that it's a selling job of some sort and the more you sell the more you'll get paid.

COMMISSION ONLY Also sales. It means you'll get nowt unless you sell tons of whatever it is they make or do. Approach with extreme caution. You're potentially in scamster territory again.

SALARY UP TO Usually a very high figure. Again the ad should give you a clue. If it's a reputable-looking outfit then they are probably genuinely looking for someone special and prepared to pay top whack for the right person. On the other hand a less august ad could mean that that figure is what the boss earns, and until you get that job, you'll be on significantly less.

TIMING

Once you've got a broad idea from looking at the advertisement of what the job actually is, what it pays and whether or not you can do it, you have to work out how quick off the mark you need to be. Which means taking a look at exactly why an organisation advertises a vacancy in a newspaper. The first reason is the mandatory one. All local or national government departments, and many other official bodies, have a policy that their vacancies should be made widely available to all jobseekers via the media. Their recruitment policy will also dictate that there is a long cut-off point for applications, that they all must be looked at and usually that each and every applicant be notified. This means that there is no rush to get your details in. Just check when the closing date is, cut out the ad and keep it for when you're not so busy, and you can devote the necessary time and care to making a fantastic application. Then bung it in and be prepared to wait a long time before you hear anything.

For many companies in the commercial sector, taking an ad in a paper is a last resort. They must have had no luck promoting from within or in headhunting (i.e. poaching someone from another company), no one in the company could recommend a person and they haven't got your details already on file. So they have to go to all the time and expense of booking the space, designing it, writing it and paying for it. Then the real work starts. A job ad in any paper, local or national, generally leads to a massive influx of mail – much of it from entirely unsuitable people – which has to be sorted, sifted and responded to. Then there's the trauma of interviewing, selecting and finalising candidates. It's all time and money that most employers would rather dedicate to something much more directly productive.

In which case you could forgive them for seizing on the first one or two that drop through the letterbox who look as if they're qualified, able and available. Which is why in those cases it is imperative that your envelope is the first to hit the mat. Which means that you need to see the advertisement before anyone else.

Here's a list of the types of publications that carry situations vacant and some hints on how you might get your paws on them before the rest of the rats:

LOCAL WEEKLY Either as a freesheet or proper paper, you'll find it available at the newspaper's offices before it ever gets through your letterbox or into the newsagent. Sometimes as much as 24 hours beforehand.

REGIONAL DAILY Again, if you live near their offices, you'll see it there first. A lot of 'evening' papers actually come out in the morning now. Just call in and ask, 'When does the paper arrive?' If you don't live near the office, street vendors usually get theirs before the shops do.

NATIONAL DAILY Get up early. Very early if you like. In fact you might not go to bed. In some cities daily papers are available at midnight. Failing that, it's worth checking what time 24-hour grocery stores and petrol stations get them delivered.

NATIONAL WEEKLY If the paper or magazine is based in London, and most of them are, then in some cases the capital gets them before the rest of the UK. You could go and get them yourself, but that wouldn't be sensible if you live in Inverness. Do you have a friend in London who could get it for you and then read out the relevant jobs over the phone? If you've got access to a fax machine, that would be even better.

TRADE AND SPECIALIST Ring up the Subscription Department and ask them what day the publication hits the street, and whether you get it any earlier as a subscriber. If you do then you should speak to your librarian. Most of their magazines come via subscription. An extra day could give you a real edge.

Cut out and keep for reference all the jobs that you intend to apply for (not the ones in the library, photocopy those!) and then prioritise them into the urgent and the non-urgent. If you stand any chance of getting an application to a firm that day, then take it. If they're local to you, there's no reason why you shouldn't go down there and hand your application in at the premises. One employer told me he hired someone who had called in to ask for an interview for a job he'd seen in that day's paper, before the employer had even realised the ad had gone in. Failing that, it's good old-fashioned first-class mail.

MAKING CONTACT

Before you put anything in the post you could try giving the company a call. Some ads will positively encourage you to do this, but even if they don't it's worth a shot. Identify something that you'd really like to ask about the job, phone the contact and explain that you've seen the ad, you're interested in the position, and can they just tell you how much actual widget wibbling you'll be expected to do? It gives you an opportunity to make a vital contact, before anyone else; perhaps you'll get on dead well and they'll remember you. When you send your application in you could say something like 'Further to our telephone conversation today' or 'Thank you for outlining your widget wibbling schedules yesterday; it has prompted me to apply for the job'. That should jog their memory. You could also enquire whether it would be possible to fax or email your application. That way you get there faster than anyone.

If there are jobs in your pile that you're unsure about and you have the time, then there's no reason why you shouldn't apply anyway. It will give you an opportunity to brush up on your application and interview skills. In that by now familiar 'increasingly competitive job market' recruitment and selection techniques are constantly changing, so it will keep you abreast of modern methods and help to make sure that your interview tecnique doesn't get rusty.

THE VOLUNTEER BUREAU

If you really want a job, of course, then there's a whole load of people out there who will give you one. Provided of course that you don't expect to be paid for it. Now, who would want to get involved in that kind of palaver? Mug's game isn't it?

Well, what else are you going to do? Think about it. If you are out of work the chances are that you may be looking for a job for some time to come. Attractive though the delights of daytime TV and endless DIY opportunities might be, they're not going to provide you with a whole lot of mental stimulus are they?

Volunteering may just prove to be the solution to a lot more problems than you at first imagined. Obviously a lot of people will volunteer to do things for good causes for worthy and altruistic reasons. It gives them a warm and fuzzy glow born of doing good works for the sake of it. And good on them. You however are going to have to be a little more pragmatic about your motives. You want to get a job. And volunteering could well be a useful and enjoyable way of helping you secure one.

Let's just dispel a couple of misconceptions to begin with. Contrary to some people's expectations the voluntary sector is not solely the province of genteel ladies of a certain age beavering away in charity shops and soup kitchens. All sorts of people from all walks of life nowadays get involved in a huge array of activities. In 1999 there were over 3 million people working for around 135,000 UK-based voluntary organisations. The choice of activities is as vast as those in the actual job market.

And don't for one minute make the mistake of thinking that voluntary organisations are all well-meaning but ramshackle outfits run by fuzzy-minded do-gooders. Most are in fact highly professional organisations with sophisticated training programmes and excellent working practices.

Aside from the lack of wages, volunteering is very much like getting and having a job. If you've been out of work for a while or have yet to start your first job, you can think of it as a dry run. Many of the more switched-on voluntary organisations even run ads in the situations vacant columns of the local paper, so you'll even be looking in the right place.

In the first instance you'll probably have to submit an application form and attend a formal interview. There'll be some sort of selection process. Even though a lot of organisations will be crying out for help, they won't want the assistant village idiot on board or indeed some screwed-up psycho from the planet Weird. So this is your opportunity to practise and hone your interview skills.

In the second instance you will be making a commitment to go to a certain place at a certain regular time and you'll be expected to perform some sort of task along with some other people. That's what work is, pretty much. Aside from the undoubted psychological kick in the pants that having a regular responsibility should give you, you'll be doing stuff. Stuff that may well stand you in good stead for the future.

Not only may you be picking up new experiences on the job, and we hope learning from people experienced in the field, but any decent voluntary organisation will have the facilities for making sure that training opportunities are available in abundance. Not just within their specific field either. New technology, management skills, administration, accountancy, fundraising and counselling are just some of the many types of training that are automatically available to most people in the voluntary sector.

If you are a school-leaver or have had a long lay-off from work, volunteering also gives you an opportunity to put something on your CV other than 'interests include music and going for long walks'. And, crucially, it should be the golden opportunity to have someone other than a former schoolteacher supply those all-important references you'll need for future job applications.

If you're unemployed you can do as much voluntary work as you like. Your Jobseeker's Allowance will not be affected as long as you tell them what you're up to. Remember that you've signed that Jobseeker's contract agreeing that you will look for full-time work.

MEANING WHAT?

Volunteer bureaux are local volunteer recruitment and advice centres. Yours may also be called a Volunteer Centre, Council for Voluntary Service, Voluntary Action or Volunteer Development Agency. Almost every major town and city in the UK has one. They act as a kind of recruitment agency between you and the organisations in your local area, introducing you and helping you find the right position for your needs. They also give training, support and advice to those local organisations to make sure they are using you to your fullest potential.

The Benefits Agency expects you to be contactable at all times in case a job comes up, and in the event that it does, they expect you to be available for full-time work within 48 hours.

You can't earn any money from volunteering. Reasonable expenses

TIP
Be realistic about the hours you can give. The key is quality over quantity every time.

for travel, meals or special clothing are excepted, but anything else is considered payment, should be declared, and will affect your benefit. It is advisable in any case to take along a letter from the organisation that you're working for clearly stating the following:

● Why you're volunteering

● Any training opportunities available to you

● The hours you'll be working

● Any remuneration you'll be entitled to

● Confirmation that you can still be contacted by employers

If you go for the volunteering option you'll find your horizons broaden considerably. Not just in terms of the usual meeting people and learning new skills stuff, but also in terms of employability. You will have proved – both to yourself and to a potential employer – that you can fit into a new work environment and make the most of it. Now all you need to do is get paid for being so smart.

AGENCIES

If you decide to take this route as part of your job hunt, then you'll have no shortage of places to go. The high street and the newspapers are crowded out with employment agencies seemingly tumbling over themselves to find you work. What could be simpler than strolling into one and asking them to fix you up with a job pronto?

Sadly, it ain't that straightforward. And you're going to have to get your research head on again if you want to get to grips with the intricacies of the system. Broadly speaking, there are three types of employment agency:

● Job Centre

● Temp agency

● Recruitment agency

THE JOB CENTRE is the most straightforward and if you're unemployed you're already familiar with where it is because it's in the same building you go to sign on. If you haven't been in one, it is worth a look. Basically you'll see long rows of boards clearly marked with the kind of job they carry. Part-Time Work,

Engineering, Secretarial and Clerical, Retail, are just some of the selections available. On each board there is a series of cards, each containing the details of a specific job – usually a description, the hours, the pay and any qualifications required. There are no contact details. What you do is make a note of the job reference number and take it along to a member of staff.

They will discuss with you briefly what the job entails, ascertain if you're suitable and then call the employer to arrange an interview, the details of which are arranged there and then. The system functions like that so that employers aren't tied up with rafts of unsuitable people calling them up and harassing them with requests for interviews. The Job Centre actually provides a whole host of services for employers to assist them in their selection process, so a switched-on job adviser may be a useful contact to cultivate. Watch out however for the switched-off job adviser. A couple of jobseekers told me they were unhappy with the way the member of staff presented themselves – on the applicant's behalf – to the person on the other end of the phone. If you get the feeling that the adviser is a JEEP (Just Efficient Enough to Perform) you could change your mind before they pick up the phone and try later when someone more capable is available.

Really, a daily visit to your Job Centre is advisable. The vacancies are updated constantly, and it also carries a selection of newspapers as well as leaflets and information on current training opportunities and any special schemes that may be in place.

Job Centres are run by Employment Services who also run a phone-line information service on 0845 606 0234. It's called Employment Services Direct and can be quite a nifty way of tracking down a job. You speak to an adviser who has access to a mainframe computer which is linked to every Job Centre in the UK. They can do a search for you either by location or job title. If you've now made up your mind that you're definitely going to be a lion-tamer and you're prepared to work anywhere in the country to follow your dream, the adviser can punch in 'lion-tamer' and within seconds will be able to tell you where all the vacancies are. The line is open until 6 pm each day, and the calls are charged at local rate.

The other types of agency are all profit-making entities. Someone, supposedly the employer, is paying to keep them in fancy matching office furniture, so as with all other commercial services, you need to do some market research.

MEANING WHAT?

The Department of Trade and Industry (DTI) draws a distinction between an 'Employment Agency' and an 'Employment Business'. In their eyes an agency is there to get you permanent work. If they succeed they get a fee from your new employer. They are not responsible for you in any other way. All your tax and National Insurance matters are dealt with by the employer. An Employment Business is supposed to get you only temporary work, and if they succeed then they become your employer. The company you worked at pays the Employment Business and they pay you. The agency issues the P45 and they deduct any tax or National Insurance contributions. It's what we as lay people would refer to as a 'temp agency'. Confusion can arise because most companies working in recruitment will have two arms to their business, complying with both sets of regulations but working under the generic title of an 'agency'.

All employment agencies or employment businesses are licensed by the government through the Department of Trade and Industry. As such they have to abide by a number of rules. In theory, the penalties for breaking those rules can be quite severe. But like any other dodgy operator, an unscrupulous agent can work out how to either live within the rules or find a way around them.

For your protection and information here's a rundown of some of the key rules pertaining to jobseekers that agencies are supposed to abide by:

- Employment agencies and employment businesses are prohibited from charging fees to workers for finding or seeking to find them jobs.

- Employment agencies must not offer workers financial benefits or benefits in kind to persuade them to use their services.

- Employment agencies proposing to charge a worker a fee for services other than job finding must, before providing such services, give the worker a clearly legible written statement detailing the service and the proposed charge.

- Employment agencies must not make the provision of job-finding services conditional upon the worker using their other services.

- If an employment agency receives money on behalf of a worker client it must pay it directly to the worker within ten days of receipt or, if the worker has requested the agency in writing to hold money received from employers on the worker's behalf, must pay it into a special client account operated in accordance with rules set out in the regulations.

- An employment business must give to a worker on entering its employment full details in writing of the terms and conditions of employment, including whether he or she is under contract of service or is self-employed, the kind of work he or she may be supplied to do and the minimum rates of pay for such work; subsequent changes agreed by the worker must also be given to him or her in writing.

- An employment business must give the worker all available information about the nature of the hirer's business, the kind of work and the hours and rate of pay applicable, and make appropriate inquiries to find out whether the worker has any qualification that is required by law for the work and that performance of the work (whether in the UK or abroad) will not contravene the law.

- An employment business must not prohibit or restrict its workers in any way from entering the direct employment of a hirer and must not refuse to pay a worker because it has not been paid by the hirer.

TIP
Au pairs going to work abroad can be charged an agency fee but it should not exceed about £40.

There are some exceptions to those rules. Anyone working in showbusiness, the arts or as a model can be charged by an agency for finding them work, usually on a commission basis.

Remember that the primary purpose of any agency is to make money. The respectable and professional ones will take the long-term view that the better they look after their clients the longer they'll stay in business. There may be others who don't really give two hoots about how long they stay in business so long as they make a pile of money for the duration. You have to try and suss out which is which. Note that one of those rules states that if they are going to charge you for something other than finding you a job, they must make clear what it is.

That means that there is provision even under the law for them to hit you up for some money. The most common services offered include professional CV writing services, careers counselling and a whole panoply of special tests that might just lead you to believe that you're best off applying for jobs that they happen to have a lot of vacancies for. It's entirely up to you, but can you really afford to shell out on something that we've proved you can do yourself?

TEMP AGENCY Dealing with a temp agency should be fairly straightforward. You sign up and they find you work with employers who need people on a part-time or casual basis. You do the work and a cheque turns up. There are one or two out there who recognise that their clients are strapped for cash and they'll even pay you on the day you work. Don't expect massive wages. The national minimum wage is rarely exceeded unless the circumstances are exceptional or you are a professional signed up with a specialist agency. There a whole load of these dealing with teachers, medical staff, accountants etc. They are well worth signing up with if you do have professional skills or qualifications: in an emergency an employer will call an agency as soon as they've exhausted their personal contacts.

If everything goes horribly wrong with a temp agency it's dead easy to just stop taking work off them and start harassing them for the money they owe you.

RECRUITMENT AGENCY Recruitment agencies can be a little trickier. You look in the window, or at their advert in the paper, and you'll see that they've got hundreds of exciting opportunities with dozens of employers who are screaming out for staff. You stroll in there and you find that they have nothing for you. How can that be? You have to remember that they are paid a commission by the company for finding employees, usually based on the first year's salary. Given the choice of 10 per cent of a widget wibbler's salary and the same tithe from the executive head of wibbling, which would you take?

A lot of those ads are designed to make them look attractive first to anyone who might be an unemployed executive head of wibbling, and second to the employers, who are really the main prize here.

There's an infinite number of job hunters but there's a lot of recruitment agencies chasing a comparatively small amount of business. You might be in there pouring your heart out and trying to explain why exactly you were born to tame lions and they couldn't care less. Sure, they'll put your details on file, but they'll get a call from a circus looking for staff about as often as Porky Pig dons his flying jacket. Now if you were an IT specialist, that might be a different matter. Big companies need those guys and fast. So they'll follow the money every time.

Perhaps the best way to deal with agencies is as just another part of your overall strategy. Check them out and if you like their style and have a good feeling about them, let them keep your details and who knows? They obviously do get people jobs otherwise they wouldn't stay in business. But you'd certainly be ill advised to sign up and then go home to play computer games until they phone with a job. Your thumbs may well have fallen off by the time that happens.

When you do sign up they may try and indicate that pursuing your own job hunting will prejudice their professional endeavours on your behalf. Act dumb. Smile sweetly, nod politely and carry on exactly as you were. They may want that commission to pay some overhead, but you need that money for the rest of your life. It's not worth the risk. Especially don't tell them about any specific leads you've developed. Tell them nowt. If they know you've been hanging out with Mr Sludge at Corpameg and he's promised to bear you in mind next time something comes up, they will dive in there and try to exploit your lead. Don't fall for any nonsense about 'exclusivity' either. They're just trying to stitch up the labour market in their corner of the world. If they tell you that you'd be advised to just stick with the one agency, act dumb. Nod politely and smile sweetly. Repeat smiling and nodding at all the other agencies you sign up with. If there is more than one agency in town they'll be dealing with different employers anyway. You can't afford to limit your options.

Occasionally you'll come across an employer who will stonewall you completely when you try and enquire about vacancies. They'll insist on directing you to their recruitment agency, insisting that they never hire unless it's through them. It probably isn't strictly speaking true. If the managing director's nephew was looking for a gig, they wouldn't make him schlepp all the way down to the

TIP
The bulk of the specialist agencies are based in London, so you'll need the relevant Yellow Pages.

>> p94

Networking skills

agency now would they? So refer back to the bits on networking and get your research head on. But it will mean that you may have to deal with the agency.

In which case stay on their case. In this whole book I hope we've stressed that you should never harass an employer to the point where you become a pain in the ass. Now you can break that rule. Call them up and ask for news. Call them up and ask them when would be a good time to call them up again to get the news. Call them up and ask them if you can call in and have a chat about the news. Call in have a chat and tell them you'll call them up tomorrow to see if there's any news. Even if they dodge you, your name will constantly be at the top of their message pad. They'll want rid of you in the end. And the best way to get rid of you is to get you a job. Just make sure they never forget you.

If you ever feel that you've been treated badly by an agency, or believe that they have broken the law, then you should ring the Department of Trade and Industry and ask for advice. They have a special helpline on 0845 608 1122 which deals with complaints and enquiries about employment agencies. Call them even if you have no proof but just feel that you've been the victim of some sharp practice. The DTI monitors dodgy agencies and the more people who complain about them, the closer they'll get monitored.

THE INTERNET

This is not a book about the internet so we're not going to spend any time here defining it, explaining it or providing any consumer research into the best internet service provider. All of that is readily available on the newsstands. Plus which, if you know about it then you don't need a techno-klutz like me stating the obvious and denying you precious surf time. This is the merest glimpse at the workings of the thing with a special slant on how it pertains to job hunting.

If you haven't used the internet then you need to get online and fast. Don't worry, it's not some big, scary complex thing which is going to throw 24-hour-a-day pornography at you and steal all your money. It's like being in the biggest library in the world, with every librarian in the world scurrying back and forth bringing you information as soon as you tell them what you want. It's also one of the quickest and cheapest ways to communicate with anyone in the world.

You don't need a computer to get webbed up – try the local library, resource centre, college, one of the internet cafés or an amiably accommodating chum. A chum's machine is perhaps the best way to learn about the internet. Logging on really is like falling off a log and it's the kind of thing that you get familiar with by doing it yourself. A chum can start you up and then let you get on with it, until one of those odd things that only happen in cyberspace crops up. Then your friend can reassure you that everything is cool and you can get back to it.

Email, or electronic mail, is the system whereby messages can be passed anywhere around the world within seconds. If you've got it then you're one step ahead of all those job hunters who haven't. It's useful for contacting employers, sending application forms and submitting your CV. You can open a personal email account from any computer. You get your own password and user name so that it's secure and you're able to retrieve your mail from any other computer.

What we're going to do here is concentrate solely on those areas where the internet can directly help – and in some cases hinder – you when it comes to jobseeking. There are four main areas that you need to be aware of:

● Research

● Advice

● Job postings

● Networking

RESEARCH is where the internet scores the most points over any other aspect. It was originally devised by the American military for reasons that remain largely shrouded in myth and conspiracy theory. But it really took off when it was appropriated by academics as a way to pool research and communicate their findings. Which means that at its core the whole thing is based on the ethos of gathering and sharing information.

A dedicated jobseeker would be well advised to take advantage of

Basic stuff

this state of affairs. If you cast your mind back to the section on research skills you'll recall the importance of finding out as much as you can about a company before you approach them for work, or to attend an interview. Well, the internet's the place to go. In the first instance even small companies and organisations have their own website these days. Most of what you see there will be simply selling stuff, but they usually include a history of the company along with full contact details and in many cases a list of vacancies. With a little ingenuity and experience you can even track down current or former employees dishing the real dirt on company policy and personnel in no uncertain terms.

The second really useful area lies in the amount of print media that exists as an online facility. Pretty much every local, regional and national paper has an electronic version out there in cyberspace, as do many of the trade and specialist rags. Some of the nationals carry lists of current job vacancies that are updated on an almost constant basis.

Probably the best feature in this field though is the facility to look at local papers from around the UK – or indeed the world – most of which include jobs in their classified sections. You have the added advantage of being able to find out all the other stuff that you might need to know if you were thinking of moving house to get a job.

ADVICE The internet is full of people offering advice and just like in real life many of them want something in exchange. And that something will be money. And just like in real life the quality of the advice is variable. Careers advice seems to be a real growth area on the net. From the moment you first log on you'll notice that – perhaps disappointingly for some – far from being bombarded with pornography, you're bombarded with jobography. CV services, personality tests, consultations and all the usual paraphernalia are there in abundance. The best places to go for solid, free advice from career professionals, however, are the sites run by the major universities. They invariably carry pages written by specialists as a service to their students. Obviously it's primarily aimed at graduates out in the big bad world for the first time, but the bulk of what they have to say holds good for the rest of us too.

JOB POSTINGS When it comes to looking for a specific job the internet can be a nightmare. You have to be really careful that the potentially addictive nature of the medium doesn't mean that you end up doing all your job hunting online. There are just too many vacancies, or 'postings' as they're known, for you to look at. Even by judicious search and elimination methods you can end up totally overwhelmed by the avalanche of vacancies. Factor in the notorious lack of speed when moving from one place to another, and the myriad other distractions that lie online, and you potentially have a long and fruitless time ahead of you.

You'll eventually find that a lot of the sites duplicate information anyway. It seems perfectly acceptable for companies to lift wholesale the lists from other sites and include them as their own. And given that it's supposed to be the most modern of technological revolutions, there's a hell of a lot of job vacancies that are out of date. Some by several years. If you do decide to look for work online then it's probably best to allocate some time each week specifically for that purpose.

For certain jobs, specifically those in information technology, the internet definitely is the most popular and effective method of both searching and applying for jobs. As yet the rest of the working world has some catching up to do. Chances are though that situation will change, and perhaps quite quickly, so best to get skilled in the use of the thing now in the event that you need it in the future.

SEARCH ENGINES or directories are the little librarians that go and get the information that you need. There are hundreds of these sites, but the best of them link up with other engines to get the stuff to you. You type a key word or words into a little box, the librarians scurry around for a couple of seconds and then a list appears which details all the sites they found, complete with direct links. The first time you do this you'll type something, say 'lion-taming', and they'll proudly tell you they found 6,290 sites for you to look at. And you think 'Gulp'. But don't worry, you'll soon realise that the librarians aren't too bright and you have to explain everything to them very carefully. Most of the sites they brought you will just mention the word 'lion'. The help menu that accompanies each search engine will advise you on how to speak to them so they understand exactly what you want.

Basic stuff

There are sites that offer a tailor-made service whereby you post your CV on their pages and they match you up with an employer.

They'll even email you as soon as a vacancy comes up that matches your criteria. Theoretically that's a brilliant idea. In practice however you must remember that you are one of thousands, possibly millions who are sitting at home and logging on, hoping that their dream job will some day pop into their inbox. It may well happen, but strictly speaking that's not 'looking' for a job, it's hanging about at home hoping for a job. And as we've seen it's the jobs no one else knows about that are the best ones to target. You also have to be aware that the internet is dominated by the Americans. So you have to ensure that any posting, searching or registering isn't going to just bring you a whole load of exciting opportunities in Hicksville, Wisconsin.

NETWORKING Another real strength of the internet is its networking opportunities. Experts and wise guys love the net and the opportunity it gives them to share their knowledge, many of them with boundless generosity. If you're interested in a specific career or particular company, then head off for one of the thousands of newsgroups, mailing lists and forums that are in operation covering every subject you can think of and get yourself joined up. That way you can not only research information, but also make contact with many other people interested, and sometimes influential, in that area. They have the added advantage for the shy among us that you are making contact without ever having to speak to anyone or look at them.

In between me writing this and you reading it, someone will probably have come up with yet another way to share information on the internet. There are no end of smart ways to receive information, talk to people and ask advice. The three main ones are the aforementioned newsgroups, mailing lists and forums. The latter two are pretty much self-explanatory terms and not too difficult to get to grips with. Newsgroups do not necessarily bring you the latest news. What you've got is a list of every conceivable subject under the sun and a bunch of people signed up to each one so that they can express their opinions, ask questions, share information and hold informed debates and reasonable discussions. About half the time. The rest of the time they engage in bitter feuds, furious rants, slanging matches and general hurling of abuse. All of which means that it's not only educational and informative but tremendous fun into the bargain.

The trick of searching, be it via a newspaper, the internet or through personal contacts, is to try to keep all current job leads active while broadening the search to encompass new ones. Only you know what job you want to do, so only you can find out exactly the most likely place to look for it. But by now you will be one mean, researching, multi-tasking, communicating administrator. Out there is an employer who really needs you.

HOW I GOT THE JOB: *I did a whole lot of research about the service. I spoke to loads of people. I went down to the building and spoke to the volunteers, I did lots of reading and looked at the demographics of the area. Because I'd done my homework I was able to ask them questions at the interview about things that I'd found out. There was a lot of stuff that I'd done that obviously other people hadn't, and I think that homework was a major factor. Then when we got halfway through the interview I got them laughing. When they asked what my weaknesses were, I said 'Thornton's chocolates'. It was bit of a ploy really that I tend to use on every interview. It lightens the mood and makes you more human. It also means that they're not really concentrating on your weaknesses when you start talking about them.*

Sharon, volunteer coordinator

There's a site called **www.thesite.org** which has an excellent section on volunteering in general. It also offers a very specific service that can match just about anyone up with any position. In the standard on-screen form you merely enter your postcode, the distance you're prepared to travel, the hours you're available and the type of thing you're interested in. The site then conducts a search and gives you a list of what's available within those parameters, complete with contact details and links where applicable.

READ THIS
The Guardian Guide to the Internet. Jim McClellan. Fourth Estate. £5.99

There is a ton of books about the internet of a very high standard when it comes to guiding you through the first steps and on to more complex areas. We've chosen this one primarily because it's British. It's not that we've got anything against our friends across the ocean, it's just that they live in a different country which means that the books they write deal primarily with the concerns of their fellow Americans. Mr McClellan's book is also very well written, highly entertaining and will have you whizzing about in cyberspace with a minimum of fuss and anxiety.

NO WAY!

DON'T part with any money before someone will 'employ' you. That's not a job, it's a con

DON'T fall for get-rich-quick merchants

DON'T forget to tell the Benefits Agency about your volunteering if you're signing on

DON"T get involved with any agency that asks you for money

DON'T commit too much time to jobseeking on the internet

WAY TO GO!

DO be very sceptical of jobs that pay 'commission only'

DO prioritise job ads into those that can wait and those that have to go today

DO volunteer!

DO call in at that Job Centre regularly

DO start using the internet, particularly for research and networking

GO YOUR OWN WAY!

● Keep an eye open for ads that are repeated. It means they've not found anyone. You might be in with a better chance than you thought

● You could call an employer to discuss the job before you apply

● Apply for jobs you don't really want, to get used to the routine.

● Given the opportunity it's much faster to fax or email a job application

● There's nothing wrong with signing up to loads of agencies

TEN TASKS TICKED OFF

Asked a friend to show me around the internet ❏

Opened my own email account ❏

Found out where the local paper gets delivered first ❏

Been to the library to see which trade and specialist rags they have ❏

Went to the volunteer bureau and enquired about positions ❏

Checked out the Job Centre's latest vacancies ❏

Phoned the Employment Services Direct hotline on 0845 606 0234 ❏

Checked out all the recruitment agencies in the area ❏

Logged on and found newsgroups concerned with the field I want to work in ❏

Read a trashy magazine while taking a long hot bath. I deserve it ❏

8

WRITING
SKILLS

✳ LETTER WRITING

✳ CURRICULUM VITAE

✳ APPLICATION FORMS

I have made this letter longer only because I have not had time to make it shorter. – Blaise Pascal

The very first thing that many potential employers will ever learn about you will be from your initial letter, CV or application form. If it arrives in a dog-eared, recycled envelope stuck with sellotape, and is scrawled badly on a tatty bit of scrap paper, they're not going to think much of your presentation skills. They'll be forgiven for thinking that you are a sloppy individual with slapdash working practices. So getting this part right is of paramount importance.

LETTER WRITING

If there is one golden rule that should be running through your head as you tackle this topic it is 'less is more'. Assume that everyone you write to is very busy. The chances are that if they've advertised a position they are going to be even busier, as the groaning postman empties a bulging sack every day into their inadequate letterbox. We'll be looking at some sample content later on, but as a rule of thumb, any letters you do send out should fit onto the one A4 page.

If there is a second golden rule – or silver rule perhaps – it should be, never, ever write anything in your own handwriting. No matter how neat and tidy your best copperplate is, it will always leave something to be desired. The only time you are allowed to break this rule is if you are specifically asked by a potential employer to do so.

HELP YOURSELF

Occasionally you might be asked to write a letter to accompany your application in longhand because the company wants to see the paper you use, your writing style or even have a graphologist analyse it. That's someone who claims to be able to ascertain what kind of person you are by studying your handwriting. If you are told, or you suspect this is the case, then you might want to get someone of the opposite sex to write the letter you dictate. Apparently it is easy for a graphologist to determine the sex of the writer, so when a specimen arrives from a bloke which was really written by a woman, it will cast doubt on the integrity of the test.

help yourself

There is little excuse nowadays for not having access to a computer to produce state-of-the-art documents. Refer back to chapter 5 for advice on where to go for such a resource.

>> p78

Computer

Companies prefer to see documents that are computer-produced for two reasons. One, it demonstrates that you have a certain degree of computer literacy. Two, it's so much easier to read. Make no mistake, if five hundred applications for a job turn up and some poor sap has to wade through them all to eliminate the non-starters, the first to go to the bottom of the heap will be the handwritten ones.

The envelope should be a smart – preferably white – self-sealing

TIP

Paper sizes range from A5 up to A2. A4 is the standard for correspondence; most filing systems are designed to accommodate that size.

affair that holds A4 sheets without too much folding. A letter that you've neatly typed and laid out will lose its impact if you've scrumpled it into a tiny little envelope so that it comes out full of creases. You should type the address on the envelope like this:

Mr E. Sludge
Personnel Officer
Corpameg Ltd
67 Mount Street
Bogswiddle
Tillet
Herts HTX 1EO

Some people, when writing an unsolicited letter to a potential employer, put 'Private and Confidential' on the letter. The thinking behind this tactic is to try to ensure that the person it's addressed to actually opens it, as opposed to some third party employed to sift through their boss's mail. It's entirely up to you, but be advised that most people in business are well aware of the ruse, and some can get annoyed by it to the point of filing your letter in the nearest waste-paper basket.

Basic stuff

EVERYTHING YOU PRINT should be in black ink using an easy-to-read standard typeface. Try to resist the temptation to use personalised notepaper adorned with pictures of pink, fluffy bunny rabbits, a picture of your baby or a lady with no clothes on. None of these are vibes that a person serious about their work should be sending out.

Spelling and grammar should be impeccable. Spelling should be no problem: if you're writing on a half-decent computer it will have a spellcheck facility gets everything spot on. Always read over a print out before you send it, though, to make sure that you don't ahve correctly spelt words in the wrong place - hear instead of here, for example.

You should pay particular attention to the correct spelling of names. People can get very wound up by any misspelling. It is perfectly acceptable to ring up and ask, 'I'm sending a letter to Mr Sludge and I wondered if you could give me the correct spelling for his surname?' Get positions and titles right as well. Some people are very precious about this, so double-check. If someone is 'Head of Resource and Personnel Development' they may get upset by a letter addressed to the 'Head of Personnel and Development Resources'.

If you have difficulty with your grammar, you should probably get hold of a simple guidebook to help you. If you're really struggling then it might be well worth considering signing up for some of those classes we looked at in chapter 2.

>> p21

Claiming and learning

The best way to sort it out, and indeed an excellent way to put your mind at rest on all aspects of any writing, is to get a second opinion. Show it to a friend or relative who has a good eye for these things and let them tell you if you've made any howlers. If you're using a computer at a resource centre, library or Employment Advisory Service then you've obviously got a wealth of expertise on tap right there.

A good tip is never to write anything and just bung it in an envelope immediately (unless it really needs to be sent quickly). Instead, when you've done your correspondence for the day, put it in a big pile and come back to it the following morning. That way you can look at it with fresh eyes. You could even try reading it aloud to ensure that it all makes perfect sense.

Always keep a hard copy of every letter that you write for any reason connected to your job search and put it in your job file. If you're writing lots of letters and sending out a good wodge of application forms, you could soon lose track of what's been sent to whom and where you're up to with each one.

At this stage you will mainly be writing speculative letters which is a similar deal to the 'cold-calling' visit or phone call we looked at in the last chapter. Many people prefer this as a way of soliciting work, particularly if they're of a nervous disposition. You should be aware, however, that if you're going to go down this road, you may have to write a hell of a lot of letters, and you may not get a proportional number of replies back.

>> p94/102

Telephone/Networking skills

Don't be deterred, though – if you target your recipient carefully and write a really classy letter, it can pay dividends. Remember that the object of this exercise is to get to the jobs that haven't yet been advertised. Have a look at the example overleaf.

Please don't copy a version of this letter each time you write speculatively for a job. One of the skills you're looking to develop

Mr E. Sludge
Personnel Officer
Corpameg Ltd
67 Mount Street
Bogswiddle
Tillet
Herts HTX 1EO

Kevin Smith
69 Smith Street
Bogswiddle
Tillet
Herts HTX 4CK
Tel: 48579 39984
email: ksmith@crashweb.co.uk

6 October 2000

Dear Mr Sludge,

I hope you don't mind my writing like this, but Albert Smith suggested that you may be able to help me. I have a keen interest in widget wibbling and would be very grateful if you could let me know about any career opportunities available at Corpameg Ltd.

I have enclosed a copy of my CV, which shows that I have:
- Five years' engineering experience
- A diploma in Basic Wibbling
- Excellent references

I try to keep up with developments in widgetry and all the research I have done indicates that Corpameg is the most exciting and innovative company around when it comes to this fascinating area. I would particularly relish the opportunity to be involved in your revolutionary new Whizzo Wibbling project if at all possible.

Perhaps I could call you next week to have a brief chat about my prospects?

Yours sincerely,

ILLUSTRATION 8   Example of a speculative letter when 'cold calling' for job leads here is the ability to write letters that conform broadly to a pattern, but are angled specifically to each recipient. This one is just a model to give you a few hints. From the top then, let's have a look at a few key points:

1 Include all your contact details. If someone wants to get hold of you, they'll have their preferred method.

2 Your address should go in the top right-hand corner. The recipient's address goes on the left-hand side. The date should go underneath it.

3 When you address someone in what is essentially a business letter, you should do so by their title. Mr, Mrs/Miss/Ms, Dr, Revd if applicable. Note the Mrs/Miss/Ms option. It's the 21st century and we're still struggling with this one. Some people really do object to being called either Mrs or Miss. So it's perhaps another case where a phone call wouldn't go amiss. 'I'm writing to so and so, can you tell me, do I address her as Mrs, Ms or Miss?' Only if you know someone very, very well should you address them by their first name.

4 If you have made a contact, and you can legitimately do so, then use it. As we saw in the last chapter, it could lead to a personal recommendation.

5 You don't have to enclose your CV. In some companies unsolicited CVs get filed in very obscure places. 'Oh goodie. More scrap paper, how healthy for the environment' is not unheard of. That's why you punch up some of your more attractive qualities in the letter, just in case the recipient doesn't even look at the CV. Some people writing an unsolicited letter will try to use the subject of their CV as more leverage for making a contact. 'My CV is available if you would like to see it. Perhaps I could drop it in for you to have a look at.'

6 Don't hide your light under a bushel. Mr Sludge will never be able to guess that you have the right skills and qualities to make a grade A wibbler unless you tell him. Using a little formatting trick like 'bullets' will draw his eye directly to that part of the letter.

7 If you're writing unsolicited letters then you've embarked on a highly proactive, go-getting strategy. Good on you. Don't bottle

TIP
Putting 'Private and Confidential' on a letter to trick the third party into letting the boss open it can annoy people and be counter-productive.

it by wimping out at the last sentence and saying something like 'I look forward to hearing from you in due course.' Seize the initiative by stating that you will contact him. And after a decent interval do that very thing.

8 Pedants will tell you that you should end a letter with 'Yours faithfully' if you've addressed a letter to 'Dear Sir/Madam' or 'Dear Sirs'. You are supposed to put 'Yours sincerely' only when you've used their name. For a futile exercise, stare at those two salutations for a little while and try to work out what earthly difference it makes. Please let me know if you find an answer. You're always going to be using 'Yours sincerely' anyway because you read the last chapter, you are now a research animal and you found out the name.

Notice all of the things that aren't in this letter. Your age, your marital status, salary expectations, detailed employment history, favourite colour and which Masonic Lodge you belong to may at some point all become relevant to you getting the job. At this point you're not finding that out, what you're doing is finding out if there is a job, and if so how do you apply for it. If you've got lucky and your letter hits Mr Sludge's desk just as he's thinking, 'Blimey, however am I going to fill that position in Sector 7G?' then he has your CV for reference and/or your full contact details.

The letter you write to accompany your CV and/or application form when applying for a job is the simplest letter of all. Take a look at this:

OFF THE RECORD

If it's a good letter I always respond. But most of them are fairly poor. We get a lot that are obviously written under the auspices of the Job Club and you can sense that there's this feeling of 'It's the government's responsibility to get me a job, so I don't need to do too much'. Occasionally, though, you'll get someone who writes a letter, and they'll call in with it, and follow it up with a phone call. Then you think to yourself, 'Well here's a person who's showing some "attack" in their outlook.' I like having people around me who show initiative and are prepared to go the extra mile. I've even been known to create a position for someone, when there wasn't necessarily an obvious need for it. Just because I could sense that they'd bring a level of commitment to their work that would benefit us in the long term.

A N Employer

Is that it? Yes it is. The only thing you probably need to be aware of is the reference point in between the address and Mr Sludge's name. Make sure that if there is a reference number and/or job title you get

Mr E. Sludge
Personnel Officer
Corpameg Ltd
67 Mount Street
Bogswiddle
Tillet
Herts HTX 1EO

Kevin Smith
69 Smith Street
Bogswiddle
Tillet
Herts HTX 4CK
Tel: 48579 39984
email: ksmith@crashweb.co.uk

6 October 2000

REF: WIBBLING POSITION. 5UIHWEQD

Dear Mr Sludge,

Please find enclosed a copy of my CV and an application form for the position of Assistant Wibbler as advertised in *Widget Weekly* today.

I look forward to hearing from you soon.

Yours sincerely,

ILLUSTRATION 9   The kind of letter that might accompany your CV it absolutely right. A larger company may well have advertised more than one position, and you don't want to end up in the wrong pile. Employers also like you to mention where you heard about the job, so that they can see which medium is most effective. If you heard about it via Uncle Bert, then say so in a sentence like this:

I understand from Mr Bert Smith that you have a vacancy for an Assistant Wibbler. Please find enclosed my CV and an application form.

You should be warned that a substantial number of the authors of all the other books on job hunting will be throwing their hands up in horror at this point. Most of them recommend that you include a paragraph, or two, or three, or four, that reinforces what you put in your CV, like this:

Please find enclosed my CV. You will see that I have five years' engineering experience with Megacorp Ltd, where I was in charge of the wobbling machine. I have just recently completed my Diploma in Basic Wibbling at Bogswiddle Technical College. I am an enthusiastic and hard-working, blah, blah, drone on and on.

We say, 'What's the point?' Mr Sludge has all your details, he doesn't need to see them twice, he's a very busy man, or he's going to make someone else very busy by instructing them to go through all the applications.

A final word on jobseeking-related letters of any kind. If you're of a maverick nature and imagine that you can write witty and erudite letters of startling originality that just scream 'Hire me! I'm so zany and coool' be advised that you will restrict your avenues of opportunity to those companies that specifically hire maverick workers. Judging the tone to suit the company is a very difficult thing to do without intimate knowledge of their specific ethos, so on the whole it's probably best to play it safe.

CURRICULUM VITAE

There is one semi-tragic irony about the CV. It revolves around the fact that it throws most serious jobseekers into paroxysms of panic, as they fuss and fret about the perfect way to present it. What to include, what to omit, how to handle any gaps, whether or not they should include their hobbies, how long it should be and how they can get the former Home Secretary to be a referee.

There is research however which shows that the average employer spends around 20 seconds looking at a CV, significantly less on an unsolicited effort. Sometimes as little as no time at all. The diligently researched exploration of hidden vacancies, use of personal contacts, proper filling in of application forms and being impressive at the interview are all of much more importance.

A dazzling and creative CV is not some kind of magic spell that automatically opens up hitherto locked doors to mystical new worlds of mythical employment. And provided you've followed a few basic rules, it's also highly unlikely that any consultant, guru or snake-oil salesman can improve it to the point where it absolutely guarantees you a job. So be very cautious about parting with any precious cash for a bit of fancy typing and a paper clip.

Of course you do need a CV. It helps to support any speculative letters you send in. Some employers demand to see one, and it's a damn good way of showing off what you're good at. It also adds to the complete package of you the potential employee as a smart, well-presented and organised prospect. So the overall impression should be of the highest standard. At a glance it should be clean, well laid out and error-free. Which means that like your letters, it should always be typed on a computer.

There's no way anyone can lay down a rule on how long your CV should be – there are too many variables – but if you're pushing into four pages, then you can start looking at ways to chop it down. The waffle factor must be eradicated completely, as should the temptation to make stuff up. Employers tend to check things out carefully these days before offering employment and you can be justifiably sacked for lying on your CV. As with your letters, the spelling and grammar must be immaculate. If you can't be bothered to keep your CV error-free, what kind of standard of work can an employer expect from you?

Pretty much every CV should include the following information, usually in this order:

1 Personal details

2 Education

3 Employment history

4 Skills

5 References

PERSONAL DETAILS

The personal details are straightforward enough. They might look like this:

KEVIN SMITH – CURRICULUM VITAE

OCCUPATION – QUALIFIED WIDGET WIBBLER

69 Smith Street
Bogswiddle
Tillet
Herts HTX 4CK

Tel: 48579 39984

Email: ksmith@crashweb.co.uk

DOB: 20 May 1970

You should only put your occupation at the top if that's the kind of work you're looking for. Otherwise, leave it out. If you have any letters after your name, including graduate qualifications, then it would be wise to include them.

The date of birth thing is optional. It is illegal in the UK to discriminate against someone on the grounds of age, but we all know that it's not beyond the realms of possibility for an employer to be swayed either way by extreme youth. On the other hand, if they're interested enough to read the rest of the CV, they're pretty much going to be able to work out how old you are.

Some people include in this section their marital status, how many kids they've got, their nationality, the state of their health and – for all we know – how often they wash their underpants. What you need to ask yourself is, 'What does the employer need to know in order to offer me the job?' Any professional bodies you may belong to that are recognised in the profession you're targeting would be good to include. And if you've seen an advertisement that says 'Healthy mother with clean knickers required', then obviously stick it in. Otherwise, less is more.

EDUCATION

The education part is a chronological list of all academic institutions you have attended and any qualifications acquired there. If your actual grades weren't all you'd hoped for then you might consider listing just the subjects that you studied and the certificates you got, as opposed to detailing any substandard grades. It might look like this:

EDUCATION AND QUALIFICATIONS

1981–86:	Bogswiddle Comprehensive School: GCSEs in Maths, English, Metalwork, Technical Drawing
1986–88:	Tillet Sixth Form College: A levels in Technical Drawing, Engineering, Lion-Taming
1988–89:	Bogswiddle College of Education: Diploma in Basic Wibbling (Day Release)
1999–2000:	Tillet Adult Education Centre: Elementary Lion-Taming, Grade One (Night Class)
CURRENTLY:	Bogswiddle College of Education: Studying Advanced Wibbling (Night Class)
COURSES:	Safe Practices in the Workplace
	Computing for Beginners
	Elementary Circus Skills

At this point it also becomes clear that Kevin has two distinct strings to his bow. He can wibble widgets and he can tame lions. While he's ultimately going to have to direct his CV towards one or the other, it can't do any harm to demonstrate that he's flexible in his approach to different ways of working as well as being willing to learn new skills.

If you haven't got a whole load of education, you mustn't be unduly worried about this section. Presumably while you weren't getting educated, you were doing something else entirely, and there will be an opportunity later to put the emphasis on your other valuable qualities.

EMPLOYMENT HISTORY

Employment history is perhaps one of the trickiest parts and can be the source of much anguish for job applicants. Basically it's going to be a list of every job you've done, usually in reverse chronological order (that's starting with the last job first). In recognition of the fact that some of us have been in the job market a little longer, it's acceptable to limit your work experience to the last five or ten years, maybe the last five significant jobs you had. Whichever takes up the least space. It might look like this:

EMPLOYMENT HISTORY

CURRENT:	Part-time courier for Speedex Ltd delivering packages in Bogswiddle area. Volunteer at Tillet Lion Sanctuary. Duties include feeding lions, cleaning cages, supervising visitors, working in souvenir shop.
1988–99:	Megacorp Engineering Ltd as Assistant Widget Wibbler. Duties included wibbling, logging all widget components, machine maintenance, assisting with training, writing weekly widget progress reports.
1986–88:	Bogswiddle Burgers, Food Preparation Operative. Duties included preparing and serving food, handling cash, cleaning preparation areas, supervising children's parties.
1984–86:	Patel's Newsagents. Newspaper Deliveries. Duties included sorting and delivering both evening and morning papers.

At this point in the CV Kevin has given the barest information on what his duties included in each job. Any showing off comes either in his covering letter or later on in the document.

Strictly speaking a man of thirty wouldn't list his work as a paper boy or student burger flipper because he'd have enough career history to warrant leaving it out. We've put it in for him to illustrate how you would approach this section if you were just leaving school or college. If you're 16 and applying for your first job, then don't worry. The employer knows where you're at. They don't expect you to have an all-singing-and-dancing career history. It is worth putting these casual and part-time jobs in there, however. In Kevin's case they demonstrate that even as a schoolboy he was reliable and organised. Later on he showed that he was prepared to muck in at any level and, significantly, that he could be trusted with money.

Poor old Kevin is actually unemployed at the moment. There's no two ways around it, and a sussed personnel person would guess it immediately. However, he hasn't used the word 'unemployed' because he'd argue that he's actually quite busy: aside from all this job hunting and retraining he's been doing, there's the volunteering and the part-time work. There's a theory that it's easier to get work when you're actually in work. For some people that may be true. But if Kevin wakes up every morning thinking, 'If only I had a job, then I could get a job,' he'd probably not bother getting out of bed.

Notice too that he hasn't given any details on how he came to be unemployed. If there's a good reason for that, it may well be something he could cover in his supporting letter. It's also information that's sometimes asked for in an application form. Just find any way to explain it other than 'I was sacked'. Here's a list of possible reasons as to why you may have left a job:

TIP
Some computers also have a 'grammar checking' facility, but these are by no means infallible.

- Made redundant
- Contract expired
- Left to pursue alternative career
- Short period of illness from which I'm now fully recovered
- Moved house to be near elderly relative
- Moved with partner who got a new job

● Needed a new challenge

● Lack of security in the old job

You shouldn't really put the following even if you would be entirely justified in doing so:

TIP

Large organisations may sort their mail by department as opposed to name. So get the title right.

Didn't like the boss Makes you appear truculent and difficult.

Wanted more money Of course you do. We all do. Ideally without having to work for it. But written down in black ink on a white page it makes you look mercenary.

Overworked Of course you were. We all are. But this one gives the impression that you may be workshy.

Probably the most common reason for a person having a longish gap in their CV is the case of the parent who took time out to raise children. Usually what happens is that they get a little older, and a little less dependent, so the parent decides to venture back into the workplace. If that's where you're at, then how you treat it on your CV is up to you. A line in your covering letter might do the job, or you could slip something into your CV like this:

1988–2000	Looked after two young children, now grown up. Was committee member of PTA. Served as Treasurer of Junior Lion Taming League.

Any other activities, part-time work or courses attended could also go in here. Some parents include some or all of the millions of things that a parent has to be skilled at in order to raise a family. There is probably a strong argument for saying that if a potential employer doesn't recognise the superb administrative, communication, budgetary, diplomatic and countless other skills that you've acquired, then they're obviously some kind of Neanderthal, throwback outfit. They're probably the kind of people who don't employ younger women either, because they believe that they'll leave after a month to have a baby. They don't deserve you frankly. Sadly those anachronistic old duffers still exist, but take heart from the fact that I spoke to several employers who make a specific point of employing parents who are returning to work after raising a family, because they believe that they are going to get a much more sensible, practical and hard-working employee.

In the eyes of the experts, listing too many jobs is almost as bad a faux pas as not listing enough. They believe it makes you look feckless, or even worse as if you have a terrible character flaw which keeps getting you fired. This can be a particular problem for those of us who are freelance or work on a self-employed basis. It shouldn't really be too difficult to fix. The best thing to do is state clearly what field or fields you have been working in and list some of the most impressive – or at least the last five or so – companies that you have worked for. If for some entirely innocent reason you have had loads of jobs, then again just list the five or so most important, and leave the dates out altogether. Any long-winded explanations that you may feel obliged to supply are best dealt with in a covering letter or, even better, at the interview.

SKILLS

When it comes to listing your skills, you can approach it in a variety of ways. Some people like to write a short paragraph that outlines their achievements, strengths and areas of expertise. That's fine, but just remember the waffle factor and bear in mind what we said earlier about how few employers actually read the whole of a CV. Something like this could do the trick:

SKILLS AND ACHIEVEMENTS

I received the very highest grades in my Widget Wibbling exams, and as a result of my enthusiasm and interest in widgets was selected out of 600 candidates to be Trainee Wibbler at Corpameg, where I was promoted to Assistant Wibbler within a record time of just three months. During my time at Corpameg I achieved an average of 98 per cent widget accuracy, which is 10 per cent higher than the national standard, and was consequently given responsibility for training new wibblers.

Another nifty way of doing it might be to bullet-point your key skills like so:

CAN DO THE FOLLOWING VERY WELL:

● Wibble widgets

● Supervise staff

● Meet deadlines

● Organise schedules

● Research information

● Write reports

ACHIEVEMENTS INCLUDE:

● Increased production of widgets by devising new schedules

● Saved money on widget waste by training staff to wibble more accurately

● Achieved highest marks of any wibbler in my day release class

Remember throughout that you're a fierce competitor in that famous 'ever increasingly competitive job market'. As such, you need to look for every opportunity to sell yourself and your talents. Don't be afraid to blow your own trumpet.

You would also list under skills any languages you have – provided you really can speak them well – the status of your driving licence, and first aid or any other short courses you have completed. Don't forget to mention your newly acquired computer skills either.

Sort of related to skills are hobbies and pastimes, which traditionally go at the end of the CV. It's another area that has experts debating like over-excited politicians at election time. The crux of the debate centres mainly on the argument that if you put down too many exciting but time-consuming interests, the employer will think you haven't got enough time to work. On the other hand, if you just put 'Watching the telly' they'll think you're an inadequate human being with no social skills or initiative. I'd venture an opinion on this. Leave them out altogether. They're only going to take up valuable space, and most employers aren't going to take a decision based on your love of antique plates or extensive shoe collection unless of course it's relevant to the job.

REFERENCES

The final part of the document concerns references. The lovely things that two former employers are going to say about you that are bound to land you the job of your dreams. It's another angst-ridden area for jobseekers. But at this stage you may not even have to address it. You could just put 'Excellent references available on request.' Employers appreciate that you may not necessarily want your referees to be contacted without you notifying them anyway. So that could buy you some time.

The chances are that you will need references, most likely once you've been offered the job. All you need to do is find two people, preferably who you have worked for fairly recently, that are prepared to vouch for your good character. It is both polite and sensible to ask them first, and also have a little bit of a chat about exactly what they might be saying about you!

If you're just starting out in the workplace, it is perfectly acceptable to use a friendly teacher or lecturer, but don't forget that you can also use anyone who has employed you on a part-time basis. If you're struggling to think of anyone at all who might give you a glowing recommendation, then a last resort may be someone of good character and standing in the community who appears to know you quite well. A magistrate, vicar, doctor or MP would come into that category. And of course, if you have been doing voluntary work, then whoever runs your particular project will do just as well as an employer.

Don't get too hung up about this section. A lot of employers are actually a little sceptical of glowing references from previous companies, especially if they're competitors. They also know that even the most snidy and underhanded of bosses would think twice about assassinating your character on paper for all posterity to see. So a reference tends to be seen as an extra precaution as opposed to being a crucial factor in deciding whether or not you're suitable for the job.

KEVIN SMITH – CURRICULUM VITAE

OCCUPATION – QUALIFIED WIDGET WIBBLER

69 Smith Street
Bogswiddle
Tillet
Herts HTX 4CK

Tel: 48579 39984
Email: ksmith@crashweb.co.uk
DOB: 20 May 1970

EDUCATION AND QUALIFICATIONS

1981–86:	Bogswiddle Comprehensive School: GCSEs in Maths, English, Metalwork, Technical Drawing
1986–88:	Tillet Sixth Form College: A levels in Technical Drawing, Engineering, Lion-Taming
1988–89:	Bogswiddle College of Education: Diploma in Basic Wibbling (Day Release)
1999–2000:	Tillet Adult Education Centre: Elementary Lion-Taming, Grade One (Night Class)
CURRENTLY:	Bogswiddle College of Education: Studying Advanced Wibbling (Night Class)
COURSES:	Safe Practices in the Workplace
	Computing for Beginners
	Elementary Circus Skills

EMPLOYMENT HISTORY

CURRENT:	Part-time courier for Speedex Ltd delivering packages in Bogswiddle area. Volunteer at Tillet Lion Sanctuary. Duties include feeding lions, cleaning cages, supervising visitors, working in souvenir shop.
1988–99:	Megacorp Engineering Ltd as Assistant Widget Wibbler. Duties included wibbling, logging all widget components, machine maintenance, assisting with training, writing weekly progress report.

ILLUSTRATION 10   Stuck together, Kevin's CV actually looks like this

1986–88:   Bogswiddle Burgers, Food Preparation Operative. Duties included preparing and serving food, handling cash, cleaning preparation areas, supervising children's parties.

1984–86:   Patel's Newsagents. Newspaper Deliveries. Duties included sorting and delivering both evening and morning papers.

CAN DO THE FOLLOWING VERY WELL:
- Wibble widgets
- Supervise staff
- Meet deadlines
- Organise schedules
- Research information
- Write reports

ACHIEVEMENTS INCLUDE:
- Increased production of widgets by devising new schedules
- Saved money on widget waste by training staff to wibble more accurately
- Achieved highest marks of any wibbler in my day release class

EXCELLENT REFERENCES AVAILABLE ON REQUEST.

APPLICATION FORMS

Our whole lives are blighted by the filling in of endless forms and this can be one of the most irritating and certainly time-consuming aspects of looking for a job. There are few crumbs of comfort to be offered on the subject other than to say that once you've done half a dozen, they do get a little easier. It is impossible to overstate their importance in the process of getting a job, however. The application form is your front line of attack. Their whole purpose is to weed out the unsuitable before they ever get to the interview stage. So you must pay very close attention to how they look and what you include.

A lot of what goes into an application form duplicates the information on your CV, so you should obviously keep that document by you every time you fill one in. That means that you should also take a copy of your CV with you whenever you go for a job interview, because you may be asked to fill out forms on the spot.

Some employers don't even want to look at your CV, they like to trust the layout and line of questioning in their standard form. By all means enclose a CV, but look out for those forms that explicitly request that you don't send one. And never write 'Refer to CV' in any part of a form. That's what they put the boxes there for. Besides, your CV may have been binned at the earliest opportunity, leaving you at a distinct disadvantage.

Application forms vary quite a lot in length and content, ranging from a single sheet with bare minimum details required, up to eight- or nine-page epics that would make a good starting point for writing your memoirs. There are things that they all have in common though, and there are certain good practices you'd always be well advised to follow.

When the form turns up in the post, the first thing you need to do is read it and reread it. You need to be absolutely clear about everything they want from you, and you have to watch out for little foibles of the company like 'do not staple sheets together' or 'do not enclose CV'. You also need to be asking yourself in the light of what you've read, 'Can I really do this job?' Because if you can't, you'll be wasting everyone's precious time. These days the majority of applications come complete with a comprehensive job description detailing all of the qualities required from an applicant and usually the list of duties they'll be expected to perform. If you genuinely feel that you couldn't ever possibly match their criteria, then don't despair. Wait a couple of weeks until they've processed all the applications for that specific job, then write a speculative letter to your new contact outlining the skills and experience you do have, and asking if they have any other positions you might be suitable for.

Next get the thing photocopied before you even lay one mark on it. The photocopy serves two purposes: first, you can use it as a rough draft to practise on, and second, you can keep it for future reference, so that you can see exactly what you wrote before you go for the interview. Only when you've filled everything out in the duplicate, checked and rechecked it for errors and omissions (maybe getting a helpful and clever friend to check it), should you think about starting on the form proper.

At this point you'd probably be best to ignore the previous advice about typing everything. Unless you're a real computer whizz, setting a machine up to fill in an irregular form is one big pain in the neck, takes forever and leads to a massive pile of unusable paper. The majority of employers specify that their forms should be filled in in longhand anyway. So it's best writing time, or rather best printing. Putting everything into block capitals may be laborious, but it should look a whole lot better than even your best script. If you make a boo-boo, then Tipp-Ex it out rather than scrawling dirty big lines through everything.

It's particularly important at this stage to avoid the temptation to tell any porkies. A lot of organisations take the information on an application form as the basis for your subsequent contract of employment. If you've told whoppers about your wibbling you could be in trouble later. Don't waffle either. Be concise and avoid the use of any long words and obscure technical terms. Remember that the person sifting through the applications may not necessarily be the widget expert. When looking at the information required in a box, always ask yourself, 'Why would they want to know that? How would it make me a better employee?'

Take a look overleaf at this example of a typical application form to get some idea of the specifics that may be required from you.

Employment
Service

Data Protection Act, 1998
The Employment Service may put the information you give
onto a computer to assist with your application.

Produced by BCT(Forms) on 15/2/00

Application for employment

1209/1

1

FOR OFFICIAL USE ONLY	Vacancy number	Closing date
Vacancy applied for		
Employer's name	ES office stamp	
Return form to:		

2

• Where tick boxes appear, please tick all those that apply.

Personal details

1 Title   Mr ☐   Mrs ☐   Miss ☐   Ms ☐   Other ☐ ▶ *Please specify*

First name(s) _____   Surname _____

2 Address _____   3 Daytime telephone number *(include STD code)*
_____

Evening telephone number *(include STD code)*
_____

National Insurance number

Postcode

4 E-mail address _____

5 Please state driving licences held *(include any points on your licence and the reasons for them)*

6 Work history *(include any dates when you were not working)*

Employer	Dates		Position held and description of duties	Reason for leaving
	From	To		

ES5
Version 1/2000

over ▶

Printed for ES in the UK ATC990186 03/00

ILLUSTRATION 11   Employment Service form ES 5 – a typical employment application form

7 Education and training

School/College/University etc attended	Dates		Qualifications gained or course studied
	From	To	

3 →

8 Any other information relevant to your application

(continue on a separate sheet if necessary)

4 →

9 Do you consider yourself disabled under the Disability Discrimination Act *(DDA)*?   ☐ Yes   ☐ No
(If you are unsure the Jobcentre can give you information about the DDA)

Do you require any particular arrangements for an interview?   ☐ Yes   ☐ No

(please give details)

10 References

1	2
Occupation	Occupation

Declaration

11 I confirm that, to the best of my knowledge, the information given on this form is correct.

Signed   Date

1 Here's a classic example of where you should study everything on the form beforehand. You can bet anything you like that they get loads of forms where the applicant has blindly rushed in and started filling in this box. The one that says 'For official use only'. You'll find such boxes on most forms.

2 They have very politely explained that tick boxes should have ticks in them, so use ticks not crosses and don't try to squeeze tiny little words into the boxes. Think about the ones you're going to tick before you pick up your pen.

3 'Any other information relevant to your application.' This is where you should have a good look at the job description to try to determine what skills you have that could swing this job your way. Think laterally about what they call 'transferable skills'. If you're still hankering after that lion-taming job, but your experience is in engineering, then a transferable skill might be ' ability to repair all types of metal structure, including lion cages'.

Note the size of box 8. You wouldn't get a whole heap of information in there would you, especially if you're trying to write clearly. The Employment Service's invitation to ' continue on a separate sheet if necessary', should certainly be accepted. Make sure that you mark your separate sheet to identify clearly that it is a continuation of your entry in box 8. There's no point in writing out masses of relevant information if it's not crystal clear where it goes. And make sure the information is relevant, not a load of old waffle. Staples aren't usually a good idea on official forms, but do paperclip your separate sheet to the form.

4 If you are disabled, this question is by no means designed to impede your chances of a job. Quite the reverse. There is specific legislation in place to ensure that no employer can discriminate against you, and also to ensure that employers provide the facilities you require to do your job.

In a lot of cases the going rate for a job is a fixed one. Like it or lump it. If you can't live off the wages offered, look elsewhere. Sometimes there will be a section on the application form entitled 'Salary details'. They want to know how much you got paid in your last job, and how much you want for this one. Your first tactic should be to try to dodge this question if at all possible. Obviously, your new employers would like you to work as cheaply as possible. They'll have a salary figure in mind, but would be dead chuffed if they could knock it down a bit. You've obviously done your budgets back in chapter 3 and know what you need in order to live, pay your debts and buy some sweeties. Somewhere between the two standpoints there is a figure that will make both of you happy. An application form is not the best place to open those negotiations.

>> p36

Staying solvent

If you can find no way of fudging or ignoring the question then do some research on what the going rate for the job should be and quote a figure that is about 20 per cent either side of it. So if Kevin knows that the average widget wibbler gets £20,000 a year and that he could comfortably manage on a little less, he might put 'I am looking for a package worth between £18,000 and £22,000 a year.' He uses the word 'package' in case the employer looks at the figure, knows he won't pay it but offers Kevin an interview thinking that he'll accept less money but more perks, benefits, annual leave etc.

If you get an application form for a job and it throws you a real curve ball, something we haven't covered here and that you just can't figure out an answer for, then try giving the company a call. A lot of organisations will offer that option anyway, but even if they don't you can seize the initiative. Ensure that you do have specific, sensible queries, don't just ring up for a bit of a chat. You may find that the person responsible is really helpful and that you get on dead well, in which case you'll have loads of background information to prepare for the application and interview processes.

I really, really wanted to work there so I sent in my CV, which I kinda hoped they wouldn't look at too hard. I thought it showed that I was underqualified for the job, but I also sent a kick ass letter. I'm much better on paper than I am in person, and that got me an interview, where these two chicks gave me the grilling of my life. I thought I was way out of my depth. In the end I said to them, 'I don't even know how I got as far as an interview,' and one of them said, 'You wrote a really passionate and convincing letter.'

Henry, IT support worker

There are loads of websites that give information on how to write a CV or complete a job application form. Many of them will be looking ultimately to charge you a fee for a consultation or writing service. There are also a vast number of sites run by government organisations, careers services and educational establishments that offer really helpful tips and practical examples. Part of the trick of writing a good CV may be for you to look at a lot of different examples, and half an hour surfing around all of these various sites will give you a good broad perspective.

The best way to group them all together is to go to **www.ask.com** and type in 'How do I write a CV?' The groovy little butler bloke will then deliver you an easy-to-access list of results. If you get fed up with reading about 'résumés' as opposed to CVs you can click on **ask.co.uk**, and you'll get good old-fashioned British advice. Just bear in mind that a lot of what is presented as fact is really opinion.

READ THIS

Letter Writing by some other genius in the *Everything You Need To Know* stable of dazzling and informative writers. What a book! This one actually will change your life, bring you untold wealth and get you laid more often. Obviously I haven't read it, but it seemed like the best one to plug.

NO WAY!
DON'T waffle. Keep all your job-hunting documents as short as possible

DON'T leave any spelling mistakes or grammatical errors in any document you send

DON'T put 'Refer to enclosed CV' on an application form – it will annoy the employer

DON'T be modest. It's okay to show off. Everyone else will

DON'T tell lies on a CV or application form

WAY TO GO!
DO use a computer for all letters and CVs

DO ring up and ask if you're not sure how to spell someone's name

DO keep copies of everything you write

DO try to change your CV so that it's angled towards each specific job

DO read application forms carefully and follow all the instructions

GO YOUR OWN WAY!

- You don't have to include your CV with a speculative letter

- You could get a friend or relative to check all your written work for mistakes

- You could leave any letters or application forms for 24 hours before you send them. That way you'll be looking at them with fresh eyes

- It's up to you whether you include your hobbies and interests on your CV. Just remember to keep it brief

- If you're a parent returning to work, you could list all the skills and knowledge you've acquired in that role on your CV

TEN TASKS TICKED OFF

Made sure I've got plenty of envelopes and white A4 paper ❑

Practised laying out my CV on a computer ❑

Found someone to check all my spelling and grammar ❑

Asked two people if they would supply references ❑

Got hold of a decent grammar primer ❑

Wrote my CV ❑

Wrote a whole load of speculative letters ❑

Rewrote my CV and made it shorter ❑

Rewrote my speculative letters ❑

Went for a long walk in the woods. I deserve it ❑

9

DEALING WITH
THE INTERVIEW

✳ BEFOREHAND

✳ ON THE DAY

✳ QUESTIONS

✳ AFTER THE INTERVIEW

The way I see it, if you want the rainbow, you gotta put up with the rain. – Dolly Parton

We'll not try and kid you here, interviews are tough things to do. They're not the best part of job hunting by any stretch of the imagination. They can be tricky for even the most confident of people to handle. And if you're the shy and retiring type they can be a nerve-wracking ordeal. But they have to be faced because that's pretty much how anyone gets any job.

There's every chance that the first one or two you're going to screw up as a matter of course. That's part of the learning curve, and will be almost entirely down to the fact that you've never done one before, or at least not for a long time.

But know this for a fact: doing badly in the interview does not always mean that you've blown it. Sure the interview is important, but if you've paid attention to the other aspects of your job hunt and you really want the position, the employer will spot that.

Remember that whoever is interviewing you knows that you are nervous and will take that into consideration. If they have any experience or training in the field of job selection, they should be bending over backwards to put you at your ease. They need the best interview you can give so they can get the best idea of what you're going to be like to work with.

It might help you at this point to put yourself in the employer's position for a moment. There they are trying to get on with the business of wibbling widgets and making money. Suddenly they find they need more staff. Someone has had to devote hours of time to start this whole recruitment business, draft and place the ad, sift the applications, contact the recruitment agency, read the CVs, weed out the no-marks, contact the interviewees, schedule the time, prepare the questions or tests and make sure there's enough tea and milk in the fridge. Frankly, it's all been one great, expensive and time-consuming pain in the bum. If only someone would walk in there looking like the business, talking the talk and walking the walk.

So when you walk in, for heaven's sake help the poor lambs out. You need to show a little sympathy by letting them know that you can do this job, you want to do this job, you're going to stick at it and you are the answer to their prayers. Then they can sit back and relax, safe in the knowledge that at last they've found someone suitable, and look forward to a good night's sleep before getting back to the vital wibbling of widgets that has fallen so badly behind.

And don't underestimate the interviewer's nerves, especially if it's a small place and they're the only one interviewing you. They too may be the shy and retiring type, much more comfortable with widgets than people. There's every chance they've been up to the wee small hours reading a book called *The Best Way to Interview Job Applicants*, rehearsing the questions they're going to ask you and worrying about which tie to wear.

Their misery may be compounded by pressure from above. If all the candidates turn out to be completely stupid and lazy, they may have to pick the best of a bad bunch, ending up with someone who is merely stupid. In which case they'll get it in the neck for appointing the wrong person. It can be even worse for them if it's their own business. The salary for a new employee might make such a crucial difference to the balance sheet that their very survival could be jeopardised if you turn out to be idle, lazy or dishonest.

That's how badly employers need good employees. They need you. All you need to do is let them know that you're the one they need. But remember that the interview process works two ways. Sure, they're finding out if you're the one they need, but you're getting an opportunity to find out if you need or want them. Many interviewees squander the opportunity to suss out whether or not these are good people to work for because they're understandably preoccupied with making a good impression.

BEFOREHAND

Either the envelope's going to fall onto the mat or the phone is going to ring and you'll have your first interview for the job you really want. The initial buzz is fantastic. They chose you. Someone could see that you are fabulous and they want to give you a chance to earn money at it. Watch out a little for that initial rush of self-congratulatory adrenaline: it can cause you to take your eye off the ball for a minute. Which you don't want to do because this can be a crucial stage in your ongoing research, and vital to your interview preparation.

If the news came by letter then by all means jump around and kiss everyone in the room but resist the temptation to call up and confirm the details immediately. Have some breakfast first and compose yourself. It's a little more difficult when the news comes by phone, but steel yourself to sit down, grab the pen and start thinking and asking questions.

Obviously there is a whole load of stuff you need to know – where it is, the day, the time – but there are many other things it would be really useful to know that an over-excited jobseeker might let slip by. Some of those things are practical. Like these:

- Is the place difficult to find?

- How far away is it?

- If a long way, will I get expenses?

- Where's the nearest tube/station/bus stop?

- Will I need to get a cab from the tube/station/bus stop?

- Is there car parking nearby?

- Would it be possible to get a map sent?

Sod's law dictates it's the one you forget to ask about that proves to be the most crucial. So ask all those questions in a businesslike manner and write everything down, perhaps even have the above list pinned up on your noticeboard or wall, so that you remember to cover them all. If your writing's as bad as mine then it might be a good idea to type the details up so that you're not confused by your own scrawl when you actually get there.

Along with the obvious and the practical questions there are some more you can ask which will really help you get ahead of the pack:

HOW LONG WILL THE INTERVIEW LAST? Just roughly will do, but it can give you an idea of what you're up against. Anything up to an hour, and it's a standard interview that shouldn't contain too many surprises. Over that and you're likely to be dealing with testing or the 'group selection' interview.

WHO WILL BE INTERVIEWING ME? You're really trying to ascertain whether it's just one person or a panel. If it's one person then there's every chance it's the one you've made your personal contact, and you may well have some sort of rapport going by now. If it's a panel then your contact may be part of it, but there could be anywhere from another one up to five or six interviewers. The panel interview seems quite daunting, but it does have some advantages for you. It means that you should get a fairer assessment. The panel will discuss you afterwards and if there has been one person who took an instant dislike to you for no good reason, they're likely to be overruled by the majority. It also gives you an opportunity to meet more of the people you'll be working with.

WHAT FORM WILL THE INTERVIEW TAKE? The more detail you have, the better prepared you'll be. Unless the circumstances are exceptional, you should have a few days to get yourself match-fit. So listen out for anything that you may need to brush up on.

IS THERE ANYTHING ELSE I NEED TO KNOW? Now you're on a fishing expedition and a lot depends on how well you know the person on the other end of the phone. What you're hoping they'll say is, 'If I were you, I wouldn't mention that you used to work at Megacorp. Don't forget to talk about the lion-taming and the Head of Personnel is a big cricket fan so wear your MCC tie.' It might happen, but any information you can glean from this question could be vital.

MEANING WHAT?

You should get plenty of notice if you have to participate in a group selection test. They usually last at least a day, sometimes over a weekend, and are aimed at people who are going for high-powered jobs, very stressful occupations and sometimes those who want to work in the pub business. There'll be a whole bunch of you thrown together at an assessment centre of some sort and you'll be tested in all manner of exacting ways. A lot depends on the profession, but apart from written and verbal tests there may also be physical testing, role-playing and group activities, possibly designed to test things like leadership skills. Part of the selection process will include 'social activities', which means meals together and possibly even going to the pub. However much you are reassured to the contrary, make no mistake – you are still being assessed. So make sure you get your round in. And watch how much you drink!

As soon as you've hung up from that conversation get straight back on the phone and start talking to your other contacts. Tell them you've got an interview, thank them for any part they may have played in that and ask them the same question: 'Is there anything you think I should know?' It may be that professional etiquette prevents them from saying too much, but if it's a close friend or relative then the chances are you will get some valuable pointers.

After that you need to write a brief letter confirming that you will attend on the specified day at the specified time, thanks for the opportunity and look forward to meeting you. Email is a splendid way to do that. It gets there fast, it shows that you are conversant with the technology and if it gets there within minutes of the conversation it shows how keen and professional you are. It also makes you stand out a little. Very few people bother to write confirming interviews, and of those that do, hardly any use email.

If you can't make the appointment then say so as fast as possible, by phone, fax or email. A letter takes too long, and you want this rescheduled as fast as possible. If you're working, they'll understand that you have to balance your current commitments with your new opportunity. If you're out of work, it's best to give the impression that you can't make it because you're attending another interview, which of course you may well be. If not, something along the lines of a 'previous appointment' or 'another opportunity' will do the trick.

In the time you've got running up to the interview, you want to review all the information you've gathered and see if you can't gather any more. Treat it almost as if you were going into an exam or appearing on a quiz show with Corpameg as your specialist subject. Dig out the original ad, your copy of the application form, any pertinent correspondence, and set about memorising stuff. It looks particularly impressive if you can remember people's names, their positions and any little details you may have learned about them. Then you can say things like, 'Ah Mr Sludge, you're in charge of personnel aren't you? How's it going? Did you get to the match on Saturday/enjoy your holiday in Lithuania?'

TIP
If you have access to a camcorder you could film your interview rehearsals to see how you look and act.

You could also treat the exercise as a performance, which entails learning your lines so that you deliver them naturally, and having proper rehearsals. Get a friend or member of your family to act the part of the interviewer, give them a list of the questions and subjects you think you may have to deal with and get them to give you feedback on your performance. As part of that exercise bear in mind that you will be asked, 'Do you have any questions for us?' Try to find something that you genuinely want to know about the company and the job.

The day before the interview try making a practice run at getting to the place if it's near enough. Preferably at the same time as you'll be attending the interview so that you get a realistic idea of the traffic conditions or public transport difficulties. Also so that you know exactly where it is. Modern office complexes and industrial estates can be really tricky if you don't know your way around. One of the first questions you'll probably be asked on arrival is, 'Did you find

TIP

Prepare everything the
night before, just so
there's less panic if
something does
conspire to delay you.

us okay?' It looks dead impressive and shows real enthusiasm if you say, 'No problem. I made a trip out yesterday just to be absolutely sure.' Conversely, if you get screwed on the day by a bad train connection or misleading road sign, they're not going to be all that concerned about why you were late, they're just going to think, 'If he can't be bothered to get to the interview on time, what's he going to be like when he's been working here for a few weeks?'

ON THE DAY

>> p83

Clothes & appearance

Having referred back to chapter 5 to ensure that you look the part, you should head out the door giving yourself enough time to get there at least an hour before the scheduled interview. Sure you're going to be hanging around a bit if everything goes swimmingly and there isn't a leaf on the train track. But how often does that happen?

Better to be sitting in the nearest coffee shop enjoying a latte and boning up on your CV than be hurtling through the door with seven seconds to spare all hot and bothered, having spent two hours sweating in traffic on the Bogswiddle ring road.

If you haven't been able to conduct a reconnaissance mission beforehand, you may need that time to find the place anyway. Make sure you get it bang on. Walk right up to the front door and check the nameplates carefully.

help yourself

HELP YOURSELF

When you get there you may want to stick your head round the door and say, 'I'm a little early. I just thought I'd check this was the place; I'll go and have a coffee in Starbucks around the corner.' You never know. They may invite you to wait there, make you a coffee and give you some literature to look at. In which case you get to carry on with your research. An even better result is where you're so early that you catch them between interviews, or the next applicant hasn't turned up yet. So you get first shot at the title, champ. The other guy may not even be late, but he wasn't as early as you, and you will be seen as the early guy and he'll become the late guy. The one who sits in reception chewing his fingernails while you steal his thunder.

Aim to be in the place at least 15 minutes beforehand. Give yourself a once-over in the toilets ensuring that you look good and there's no latte froth on your upper lip. Then sit in reception and carry on with your research. This time can be very valuable. You may get to hear people making and taking calls, you'll see them come and go, maybe even get to eavesdrop on conversations. You might not pick up anything of staggering import in the world of widgets, but you'll get to see folk, your future workmates perhaps, in their everyday environment. Are they happy? Are they working at a good pace but without too much pressure? Are people being nice to each other? Is the receptionist obviously taking calls from disgruntled customers or hysterical creditors?

OFF THE RECORD

This is a sexy business and we get a lot of lifestyle casualties who think they can schmooze their way in with a sharp suit and dazzling interview technique. When we're interviewing we shove all the candidates into a room together, and we have someone who looks unimportant feeding them drinks and monitoring what they say. That usually sorts the men from the boys – their guard is down, some of them develop a 'spirit of the blitz, we're all in this together' approach and get garrulous. You can start to build a real picture of whether or not you really want to pay this guy to come in every day and take the mickey. I tend to go for the quiet ones who treat the quisling junior with respect and get on with reading their paper or whatever. They're usually much easier on the soul.

A N IT company director

Not only will you pick up intelligence that could come in useful during the interview but you're finding out if you really want to work there. If it's just you and the receptionist, maybe some other applicants, talk to her if she's not too busy. You should be friends by now anyway. All those calls she took from you when you were looking for Mr Sludge. But carry on with your research. How long has she worked there? Do they keep her busy? Mr Sludge seems like a really nice guy. I believe he's considered one of the best wibblers in the country. And be nice to her. In fact be nice to everybody. The interviewer knows that she may be the only person who gets to see you out of 'interview mode' and if they've any nous at all they'll ask her opinion.

TIP

The smell of alcohol lingers. Even hanging out in a bar can make you smell of drink. Perhaps best not to go drinking the night before.

At some point you're going to have to take a deep breath, walk into a room full of strangers and try to sell yourself as the perfect employee. As you cross that threshold they'll all be looking up expectantly and you have no idea what they're thinking. So I'll tell you.

They're thinking, 'Please let this be over. I hope the next one's the one. I've got work I could be doing. Please let them be at least articulate. Friendly would be a nice change. If only one of them was smart, keen and employable.'

They want you so badly. Just think how much you're going to brighten up their day by walking in dressed like the dog's wotsits, sticking out your hand, smiling and saying, 'Hello, I'm Kevin, you must be Wilhemena Squidge from the wibbling executive. Mr Sludge said you would be here today. It's a pleasure to meet you.'

Now at this point the authors of most of the other job hunting books are going to start wading in with advice about when you should sit down, whether you should accept a drink or not, how you should cross your legs, who you should shake hands with, whether you should nod your head and what to do if offered a chocolate biscuit. Blimey, you wouldn't believe what a contentious issue a humble Jaffa cake can become in the eyes of some experts. We're not going to deal with those issues. In the first instance you're a grown-up, obviously, or you wouldn't be looking for a job. You have all or most of your five senses and you have met people before for crying out loud. You'll quickly suss out the vibe and work out for yourself how to interact with these people. Second and most crucially, you've just taken a giant leap forward in securing the gig by making a good entrance. You looked great, you smiled, you were interested, you were friendly and you were hot to trot. First impressions and all that. They could see where you were coming from and there was a huge inaudible sigh of relief. You've made them happy. You can see you've made them happy, so you're happy. Everybody's happy.

Then they start in with those damn questions.

QUESTIONS

A lot of the other books on this subject come from the standpoint that interviewers ask questions to catch you out, trip you up or make you look stupid. This is probably why so many people get really wound up before interviews. But surely they're asking questions because that way they can find out what kind of person you are and if you can do the job. If there was some less painful process they'd probably do that instead, saving both of you time and discomfort.

It would be true to say that sometimes employers aren't very good at questions. Or they've got a list of stock questions that are badly in need of rephrasing. And yes there are some complete gits out there who get their jollies from making us squirm, but they're everywhere and we all have our ways of dealing with them. Faced with one at an interview you're probably going to start thinking you really don't want to work for this creep anyway.

Only the very bluntest of interviewers will directly ask the questions that they really want answering:

- Will you work hard?

- Will you stay here?

- Are you stupid?

- Are you an antisocial slob?

- Will you steal from me?

- Will you make me money or save me time?

They know it's pointless asking directly anyway. What are you going to say?

So they have to find other ways of finding out. And you have to find ways of answering those questions and putting their minds at rest. That's what they so badly want.

If you go to the library or bookshop you'll see a whole host of books that list interview questions. They'll be called things like *1,001 Answers to Interview Questions*. How dumb is that? What are you supposed to do? Memorise them all? Or sit with it on your lap, and when asked a question say 'Excuse me a moment' while you thumb through it? I bet you a pound that if you bought one of those books, you'd be asked a question that wasn't in it, by your third interview, if not sooner. Just because every job is different, every interviewer is different and you the interviewee are a unique person as well.

So what do you do? How do you answer the questions? Try this little list and perhaps use it as a mnemonic:

- Listen

- Ask

- Think

- Talk

LISTEN TO THE QUESTIONER. Give them your 100 per cent attention while they ask the question. Pay attention to absolutely nothing else except this person and what they have to say.

ASK A QUESTION RIGHT BACK AT THEM. If you understood their question then you just repeat it back. Say the question is, 'So, Mr Smith, have you had much experience with class A widgets?' You just say, 'Class A widgets?' confirming that is indeed what you're talking about. You could say this in a tone of voice that says, 'You betcha! Don't get me started on those babies, we'll be here all day.' If you're fairly sure what they're driving at but need a little clarification you could say, 'American or European standard class A widgets?' And if you really are unsure of what they're driving at, 'I'm sorry, I'm still a little nervous here, could you rephrase the question for me?' That way you don't look like a dumbo and you haven't insulted the interviewer by suggesting that their question is stupid.

THINK ABOUT YOUR ANSWER. Sometimes this will take a fraction of a second. They'll ask you something that you knew was coming up, you've prepared and rehearsed a response, so it trips off your tongue immediately. Other times you may need to give it a little thought. Of course you don't want to go into a yogic trance and start ascending to a higher spiritual plane, but there's nothing wrong with composing your thoughts before delivering your answer. Someone who thinks before they speak or act is likely to be a responsible, methodical and sensible employee. By answering some of the questions with alacrity you will have already proved that you can react fast if necessary.

TALK SENSE. Don't waffle. Answer the question succinctly, but having thought a little you should now have worked out which of these questions the interviewer was really trying to ask:

- Will you work hard?

- Will you stay here?

- Are you stupid?

- Are you an antisocial slob?

- Will you steal from me?

- Will you make me money or save me time?

Then you can go about the business of giving them the answers they're dying to hear. Be honest at all times, but don't pass up an opportunity to show off your skills and experience. If you're a modest person by nature this can be a little difficult. You might be afraid of coming across as arrogant or boastful. You can if you want moderate your showing off by using a phrase like this: 'I have to tell you that there are very few things in life I'm actually good at, I couldn't cook you a meal to save my life for example, but for some reason I have a real gift for widget wibbling. I took to it like a quacking thing to wet stuff and I just seem to get better at it the more I do it.'

If you follow the sequence – Listen, Ask, Think, Talk – you'll find an amazing thing will happen. You'll be so focused and thoughtful that before you're even aware of it, you'll become a more animated person and the nerves will start to dissipate. You may even start to enjoy yourself.

That's not to say that you may not at some point totally freeze. Nerves grip you unexpectedly and your mind goes completely blank. Oh the horror. Don't worry. It's happened to every single person who is now interviewing you at some stage in their lives. They will empathise. And they'll appreciate your honesty when you say something along the lines of, 'I'm sorry. I'm suffering from nerves a little here, I'm not used to job interviews (or, 'this interview is very important to me'). My mind's gone completely blank. I may need a moment to compose myself.'

The picture you may now have in your head is of you sitting in a chair in front of four or five lovely people seated around a table, in

TIP

Take your CV along. You may need to refer to it.

a well-appointed interview room with arty prints on the wall and a rubber plant. Which may well be the case, but beware of conjuring up that image too vividly before you go to the interview. The reality may be completely different. When Kevin goes for that job at Corpameg he may well find himself squeezed into a tiny cubicle at the back of the factory, knee to knee with Mr Sludge, whose ill-prepared and mumbled questions are difficult to hear over the roar of the wibbling machines outside the door. The phone may be ringing constantly while people keep barging in with urgent problems that only Mr Sludge can solve. It could play havoc with your focus, but be patient and use the interruptions to think about how you can best tell Mr Sludge the things he needs to know about you.

While we promised you we wouldn't burden you with a whole load of questions, it would be remiss of us not to draw your attention to a couple of things that you are almost certain to be asked sooner or later. Questions of this nature:

WHAT ARE YOUR STRENGTHS AND WEAKNESSES?

This is an old standard. It's on nearly every interviewer's list. Strengths of course are easy enough. Just paraphrase what you put in your CV. Weaknesses are trickier – you'll be afraid of saying something that might jeopardise your chances. If your weakness is that you find it difficult to get out of bed in the morning, you don't want to say so because it sounds like you'll be late every day. Perhaps the best way to approach it is to pick on something that doesn't sound too horrific, explain that it doesn't affect your work and reassure them that you've got it under control. Perhaps like this:

Well, I must admit I have a tendency to get a little bad-tempered if I'm working to a deadline and the machinery breaks down, but I am learning to take a deep breath, count to ten and resist the temptation to kick the damn thing.

Who hasn't had a machine break down on them at a crucial point? And who hasn't then broken the world land speed swearing record before giving the thing a good thump? It's not such a bad thing to confess to, and notice too that you've managed to affirm your commitment to working to deadlines.

WHY DID YOU LEAVE YOUR LAST JOB?

Or maybe, 'Why do you want to leave your current job?' Only you really know the reason why that is and whether or not you should share that information with a new employer. But there are some things you should definitely avoid saying. 'Not enough money' is one of them. As we've seen before, it makes you look mercenary and would give out a negative vibe. The other major thing to steer clear of is taking the opportunity to have a pop at your former boss or colleagues. No matter how horrendous they were. It makes you look petty and mean-spirited. Trust me on this, the first thing that goes through an employer's mind is, 'That'll be me he's slagging off in six months' time.' If really, really pushed and there's no way you can dodge the question, you could try something like:

I won't deny there was a personality clash. I don't know why and I don't know how, but we never saw eye to eye. Normally I get on okay with people so it was a bit sad really.

Shrug your shoulders and leave it at that. If you were sacked from your last job for something awful, then you've got a real problem and no amount of advice from me or any expert is going to solve it. There's no foolproof, pat answer for this one. You might want to take a leaf out of a disgraced politician's book. Many of them would take this line:

Look, I did a terrible thing there. I deeply regret it and I paid a terrible price. I lost my job, the esteem of my colleagues and quite a bit of self-respect. All I can tell you is that I have learned my lesson, big time. And I would never do such a stupid/ dishonest/immoral/illegal thing again.

HOW MUCH MONEY DO YOU WANT?

Or a variation on that theme. 'Are you happy with the salary?' perhaps. This question is really one from our list above. Probably 'Are you going to stay here?' with elements perhaps of 'Will you steal from me?' and 'Are you going to work hard?' Bearing that in mind, the best thing to do is be evasive on the specifics while reassuring them with the answer to the real question. You don't really want to be discussing the money just yet, you want to be absolutely sure you've hooked them first. If you start banging on about how much you need and expect, then it could put them off.

TIP

If you are unavoidably delayed en route, phone at the first opportunity to explain and give your estimated arrival time.

Try a variation on one of these:

I'm sure that I'll prove to you that I am worth whatever salary you can afford to pay me.

I really want to do this job, and I don't think that I'd be prepared to let the issue of the money stand in the way.

I have a good idea of what I need to live on, and I'd hope that it would match that requirement, but I think you'll find me flexible when it comes to actually discussing the terms and conditions.

I haven't given it that much thought, to be honest. I expect that you would pay me a salary commensurate with my skills and experience, taking into account my responsibilities here.

There probably really are 1,001 questions you may be asked. Possibly more. And they may be asked in a whole load of different ways. Sometimes they'll be asked in a most peculiar fashion. It's not unheard of, for example, to interview people going for high-pressure jobs by haranguing them from all directions to see how they cope. A favourite with interviewers recruiting sales staff is to pick up something obscure in the room and say, 'How would you sell me this Biro with a chewed top?'

The truth is that whatever they ask and however they ask it, all they really want to know is:

- Will you work hard?

- Will you stay here?

- Are you stupid?

- Are you an antisocial slob?

- Will you steal from me?

- Will you make me money or save me time?

You know what the answers to those questions are. All you need to do is make sure that they know how much they need you.

AFTER THE INTERVIEW

It's all over. Time to get the hell out of Dodge. But before you do that, there are a couple of things that have to be straightened out. First off, providing they haven't offered you the job there and then, you need to know when they're going to be in touch. You could also ask if it would be okay to contact them if you don't hear anything. It shows you're keen and it helps keep the contact alive. Next, thank everyone nicely and try to come up with some kind of exit line that will stick in their minds, leaving a favourable impression. It's best not to give you any ideas on this one. It should be from the heart and it should be something that only you would say. 'So long suckers' is definitely out. Don't forget to say thanks and goodbye to the receptionist, or anyone else you should be grateful to.

Now you can go to a bar. Choose one some distance from the premises though, you don't want them to see you heading in there, or indeed staggering out later. Order yourself a large one, and while everything is still fresh in your memory, replay the whole thing in your head.

And don't try to kid yourself that it was a perfect interview. You're not the Pope. Your fallibility is manifest for all to see. At some point you will have got it completely wrong. You need to identify those moments and think about how you would do it differently given your time over again. There are two reasons for this. First, so that if you don't get this job, you'll not make the same boo-boo at the next interview. Second, it may not be too late to put that mistake right.

Now you can get drunk.

The following day, having nursed your hangover and had a good think about the preceding day's events, you'd be well advised to fire off a letter to whoever interviewed you. It shouldn't be a long one, it should just thank them for seeing you, perhaps reaffirm that you really are keen on the job, and finally you should take the opportunity to clean up that little mess you made. Resist the temptation to give a complete action replay of the entire interview. Just take the one most important thing you feel you'd like to clarify and do it something like this:

Mr E. Sludge
Personnel Officer
Corpameg Ltd
67 Mount Street
Bogswiddle
Tillet
Herts HTX 1EO

Kevin Smith
69 Smith Street
Bogswiddle
Tillet
Herts HTX 4CK

Tel: 48579 39984
email: ksmith@crashweb.co.uk

26 October 2000

Dear Mr Sludge,

Thank you for meeting with me yesterday. I was very impressed by my first visit to Corpameg and would love to be offered the opportunity to work as your Assistant Wibbler.

As you probably realised, I was quite nervous at the interview. I haven't done that many, and I feel that I didn't perhaps do justice to your question about my understanding of the Series 3 Wibbling Wobbler.

While it is true that I didn't use one at Megacorp, I was trained on that machine as part of my training at Bogswiddle College. I attended lectures by Professor Claude Eustace Scrunge who developed the prototype of the Series 3 and I have, of course, studied his fascinating book *Wibbling: Whither Now?*

Thank you again for your time, and I look forward to hearing from you soon.

Yours sincerely,

The faster your letter goes the better. Email is good, as is dropping it in by hand. Who knows, you may get to bump into the employer again. Aside from the rare good manners you have shown, and the initiative in clearing up your mess, the point is that they may not have made a decision yet. How many other letters of a similar nature will they have sitting on their desk as they sift the applicants? If you could count them on one hand it would be surprising. It's another opportunity to get ahead of the pack. Even if the letter doesn't swing it your way, it shows that you are potentially one hell of an employee.

Now you make a note in your diary/day book to contact the employer a couple of days after the agreed notification time and you try to forget all about that interview and the job that may lie at the end of it. If you're a proper job hunter, as opposed to one who waits for jobs to turn up, you know you'll have plenty to do anyway. There are more situations to track down, companies to research, letters to write, contacts to be made and interviews to attend. If you do nothing but sit there waiting for the envelope to drop onto the mat telling you you've got the job, how are you going to feel if it says you haven't?

Wretched. That's how. Let's face it, you're going to feel pretty lousy anyway, no matter how many other irons you have in the fire. But if you pinned all your hopes on this one, then it's going to be even harder to pick yourself up, dust yourself down and get back in the saddle.

Look, we never led you down the garden path here. We made it clear early on that it was going to be tough, that this book wouldn't guarantee you the gig and there was every chance you would fail the first few times. So don't get too distressed. Kick the cat again, have a big long sulk and then try to get it into perspective.

Sure, it's bad news, but it ain't the end of the story. First of all, it may not be your fault. You might even have been the best candidate, given the most impressive interview and had the finest credentials. But someone else could have been earmarked for the position from the word go. And it's a sad thing to have to say, but maybe they just didn't like you. Research has been done that suggests a lot of employers make up their mind about a candidate

TIP
Remember that the Benefits Agency will pay travel expenses for a job interview if you're unemployed.

within seconds of them walking through the door. You just can't legislate for blinkered thinking of that calibre.

The second thing you have to know is that this may not be the end of your chances with that employer. If you really have put as much effort into your jobseeking as it needs then you must have been pretty impressive. The person who got the job must be some kind of superhero. Which means that the next time an opportunity comes up, they may automatically reach for your phone number. Of course you're going to send a follow-up letter anyway and try to keep the contact alive.

A lot of employers will offer you feedback on how you performed as a matter of course: if they don't, then try to get some. By doing that you demonstrate how keen you still are, and you may well get to learn something vital about yourself that will stand you in good stead when it comes to applying for the next job.

The other news that envelope might bring could leave you in a little bit of a no man's land. It could say that you've been invited back for a second interview. Now you're in a heightened state of ambivalence. On the one hand it means that you were good enough for serious consideration. On the other, you have to go through the whole rotten process all over again. Well, at least you have a good idea of what you're up against now. And it can't hurt to get on the phone and start probing those contacts again. If at all possible, you need to find out exactly what they're looking for and how you can improve yourself to ensure you stroll off with the honours.

Of course what we're all hoping is that when the envelope plops onto the mat, you open it and it confirms that you have indeed got the job. What a rush that will be. The end of the trail and the start of a whole new life. We knew they wanted you, and you were so cool and impressive that you made them realise it. Congratulations. We hope we helped you out there – you can buy me a drink next time you see me.

Now give this book to someone who really needs it. We trust you never have to look at it again.

HOW I GOT THE JOB: *I was bones of my bum skint. Totally starving to death and doing a variety of rubbish things to try to earn a crust. Every day I would spend the morning trying to find a job I really wanted to do, and in the afternoons start ringing round and writing letters. One of the people I called regularly was the publisher who commissioned my last book. We get on fine and I made no secret of my financial situation. Eventually he said, 'Look, we've got something you might be able to do.' And he offered me the job of writing a book called* Everything You Need to Know about Job Hunting. *Of course I bit his hand off. The irony being that this is a man who never had a proper job in his life. So I talked to practically every single person I know and found out exactly how they got their jobs. So I knew it would work. All my friends are in full-time employment. They wrote the book really.*

As with books, there are a whole load of sites offering advice on how to answer interview questions. They don't on the whole have much more to offer than the books, so we thought we'd cheer you up. There are lots of sites, usually from disgruntled job hunters detailing stupid questions they have been asked, and the responses they gave or wish they'd given. There's usually only a dozen or so on each page, so go to **www.google.com** which is one of the niftier search engines. Ask it to look for the phrase 'stupid interview questions' and you'll be entertained for a good hour or so. The perfect way to unwind after a hard day trying to second-guess ill-prepared or obliquely phrased questions. Two of my particular favourites from different sites are: Q: What can you say to reassure me you are aggressive enough for this job? A: Give me this job or I will kill you; and Q: How many children do you have? What are their ages? A: How many attorneys do you have? How much do you pay them?

READ THIS

Excel at Interviews. Patricia McBride. Careers Research and Advisory Service

This is quite a groovy little book, and given that it's aimed at students, the patronisation factor is encouragingly small. Ms

McBride has assembled an interesting array of experiences and quotes from real people to support her theories, and there are lots of funny cartoons to look at. She also develops areas there was no space for here that might be useful to you, specifically in her chapters on Equal Opportunities Issues and Selection Tests.

NO WAY!

DON'T panic. Stay calm when you are offered an interview. There's a whole load of stuff you need to ask

DON'T drink alcohol the night before or on the day

DON'T leave anything to chance. Give yourself an extra hour to get there

DON'T stop researching all the time you're in there

DON'T be rude or offhand with anyone. Their opinion might count

WAY TO GO!

DO use your contacts to get information about the interview

DO write to confirm you will be attending

DO rehearse beforehand what you will say

DO make a practice run the day before so you know exactly how long it takes to get there

DO try to make confident, memorable entrances and exits

GO YOUR OWN WAY!

● You could get some practice in by attending interviews for jobs you don't want

● Have a list of things you need to know about each interview, write or type them up and take them with you

● Find your own way to answer questions. If you learn responses from a book you'll just sound stilted

● Be yourself. That's who they're going to be hiring

● You don't have to take the job if you hate the place. They're on trial just as much as you are

TEN TASKS TICKED OFF

Wrote my letter confirming I would attend ❏

Used my contacts to get inside knowledge on what to expect ❏

Boned up on all the research I've done on the company ❏

Got someone to play-act the part of the interviewer
    for a rehearsal ❏

Made a practice run to make sure I know exactly
    where I'm going ❏

Prepared everything I need the night before.
    Strong liquor never passed my lips ❏

Got there nice and early. Sat in reception watching
    and listening ❏

Did the interview. Focused, asked, reflected and talked ❏

Wrote a letter of thanks and clarified something
    I'd messed up ❏

Bought a bottle of champagne. I deserve it ❏

HANDY
REFERENCE

NEWSPAPERS AND PROFESSIONAL JOURNALS CARRYING VACANCIES

ACCOUNTANCY & FINANCIAL

Accountancy	(Monthly)
The Economist	(Weekly)
Independent	(Wednesdays)
Financial Times	(Thursdays)
Money Management	(Monthly)

BUILDING & CONSTRUCTION

Building	(Weekly)
Construction News	(Weekly)

ICT

Guardian	(Thursdays)
Independent	(Mondays)
Computer Weekly	(Weekly)

EDUCATION

Guardian	(Tuesdays)
Independent	(Thursdays)
Times	(Wednesdays)

ENGINEERING

Engineer	(Weekly)

HEALTH SERVICE

British Medical Journal	(Weekly)
Guardian	(Wednesdays)
Nursing Times	(Weekly)

HOUSING

Guardian	(Wednesdays)
Estates Gazette	(Weekly)
Surveyor	(Weekly)

LEGAL

Independent	(Wednesdays)
Times	(Tuesdays)

MANAGEMENT

Guardian	(Saturdays)
Independent	(Sundays)
Telegraph	(Thursdays)
Times	(Thursdays)

MEDIA

Broadcast	(Weekly)
Guardian	(Mondays)
Independent	(Tuesdays)
Stage & TV Today	(Weekly)

PUBLIC SECTOR

Guardian	(Wednesdays)
Independent	(Thursdays)
Opportunities	(Weekly)

RETAIL, SALES & MARKETING

The Grocer	(Weekly)
Guardian	(Mondays)
Independent	(Tuesdays)
Times	(Wednesdays)

SCIENCE & TECHNICAL

Guardian	(Thursdays)

SECRETARIAL

Guardian	(Mondays)
Times	(Wednesdays)

SOCIAL & COMMUNITY

Community Care	(Weekly)
Guardian	(Mondays)

SCOTLAND (ALL CATEGORIES)

Herald	(Fridays)
Scotsman	(Fridays)

YOUR RIGHTS AT WORK

From the day you start you are entitled to:

- A minimum wage of £3.70 an hour, £3.21 if you're under 21
- Payslips detailing gross pay, deductions and net pay
- Not be unfairly dismissed for asserting your rights, raising health and safety issues or trade union activities
- Work no more than 48 hours a week
- Regular work breaks
- Time off for family emergencies
- Eighteen weeks maternity leave
- Paid time off for antenatal appointments
- Not be discriminated against on the grounds of sex, race or disability
- To be paid the same wages for doing work of equal value whether you are male or female

After two months you are entitled to:

- A copy of written terms and conditions of employment

After thirteen weeks you are entitled to:

- Four weeks paid holiday a year

After twelve months you are entitled to:

- Parental leave for children under five
- Forty weeks maternity leave

After two years you are entitled to:

- Redundancy pay

USEFUL WEBSITES & PHONE NUMBERS

WEBSITES

www.urban75.com

www.Hobsons.com

www.fool.co.uk

www.mindtools.com

www.majon.com

www.users.bigpond.com.fmcdonald/index

www.thesite.org

www.ask.com

www.google.com

PHONE NUMBERS

Career Development Loans information line	0800 585 505
Learning Direct helpline	0800 100 900
Consumer Credit Counselling Service	0800 138 1111
Directory Enquiries	192
Employment Services Direct	0845 606 0234
DTI employment agencies helpline	0845 608 1122

FURTHER READING

Welfare Benefits Handbook. Published by the Child Poverty Action Group. Reference only

UCAS Guide. Published in association with the Independent newspaper. £19.95

What Color is your Parachute? Richard Nelson Bolles. Ten Speed Press

Understanding Psychometric Testing in a Week. Gareth Lewis and Gene Crozier. Hodder and Stoughton

Dun and Bradstreet Business Register

The Guardian Guide to the Internet. Jim McClellan. Fourth Estate. £5.99

Everything You Need To Know About Letter Writing. Esther Selsdon. Harper Collins.

Excel at Interviews. Patricia McBride. Careers Research and Advisory Service